Making Multicandidate Elections
More Democratic

Making Multicandidate Elections More Democratic

.

Samuel Merrill, III

PRINCETON UNIVERSITY
PRESS

Copyright © 1988 by Princeton University Press

Published by Princeton University Press, 41 William Street,
Princeton, New Jersey 08540
In the United Kingdom: Princeton University Press, Guildford Surrey

All Rights Reserved

Library of Congress Cataloging in Publication Data will be
found on the last printed page of this book

ISBN 0-691-07770-3

Publication of this book has been aided by the Whitney Darrow
Fund of Princeton University Press

This book has been composed in Linotron Sabon

Clothbound editions of Princeton University Press books
are printed on acid-free paper, and binding materials are
chosen for strength and durability. Paperbacks, although satisfactory
for personal collections, are not usually suitable for library rebinding.

Printed in the United States of America by Princeton University Press,
Princeton, New Jersey

Designed by Laury A. Egan

TO MY FATHER
AND IN MEMORY OF
MY MOTHER

CONTENTS

CONTENTS

CONTENTS

LIST OF FIGURES

LIST OF TABLES

LIST OF TABLES

PREFACE

Choosing a winner in a two-candidate election has a simple solution: select the candidate preferred by a majority. Extending this majoritarian principle, however, to elections with three or more candidates is by no means obvious. The methods proposed are legion, may lead to quite different outcomes, and are beset by ambiguities and pitfalls.

This book uses decision theory, Monte Carlo simulations based on models of voting behavior, and reconstruction of historical elections to assess these many proposals to combine individual preferences into a collective choice. A logical approach to social choice offers insight and precision and facilitates both the rigorous analysis of known voting procedures and the design of new ones.

A mathematical way of thinking—by providing a new perspective or a new way of organizing a problem—can lend clarity to otherwise fuzzy concepts. Yet the communication of such ideas need not bristle with formulas. I have placed in appendices mathematical details that can be skipped by the reader who prefers to focus on conclusions rather than detailed derivations. This book should be readable by anyone with an interest in the consequences of electoral procedures who is willing to follow logical, quantitative arguments.

Any multicandidate voting procedure has two aspects: (1) a balloting method (specifying the nature of preferences that the voter is permitted to express), and (2) a decision rule (specifying how voter preferences are to be aggregated to determine the election result). The ordinary plurality method—commonly used in the United States, Canada, and Britain—permits the voter to designate only a first preference. In contrast, the Hare method—used in parliamentary elections in Ireland, Northern Ireland, Australia, and Malta, and New York City school board elections—the Borda count, the Coombs method, and all Condorcet completion methods (to be defined and illustrated later) require a complete preference ordering from each voter.

Approval voting, a procedure that appeared on the political scene only recently, requires each voter to perform an intermediate task—namely, to partition candidates into approved and disapproved sets. The decision rules for ordinary plurality, approval voting, and the Borda count all ascribe scores to the revealed preferences that are summed to determine a winner. In contrast, the Hare, Coombs, and various runoff methods use successive eliminations to isolate a winner.

My inquiry focuses on the performance of these and other voting procedures with regard to criteria involving the legitimacy of the outcome, the tendency of the procedures to choose centrists or to select candidates of high intensity of support, the opportunities for manipulation of the outcome, and the stability of the political system. Since all systems violate one or more of these criteria under some circumstances, the practical constitutional problem is to assess for different voting procedures the extent of these violations and their political implications.

Several recent books, like this one, address the practical applications of social choice. William Riker, in *Liberalism against Populism* (1982), is concerned with political instability due to the paradox of voting and the manipulation of social choice not only through strategic voting but also via control of the agenda. In *The Theory of Voting* (1980), Philip Straffin treats the distribution of voting power among the voters and introduces criteria that voting systems should meet by displaying examples of electorates that violate them. Steven Brams, in *The Presidential Election Game* (1978), concentrates on evaluating the implications of the present system for electing a U.S. president. In *Approval Voting* (1983), Steven Brams and Peter Fishburn focus on one promising electoral procedure, treating questions of sincerity, equity, the tendency to choose a majority candidate, and the effect of polls on elections.

In one sense my subject is the search for consensus, in large electorates, by means of the process of voting. In small deliberative groups, the quest for unity through the development of new alternatives that may be acceptable to all has been studied elsewhere by other methods (see, e.g., Mansbridge 1983, where a setting in which this type of consensus can thrive is termed a unitary democracy). I focus instead on a more constrained search for consensus among electorates in adversary democracies, that is, those in which the underlying conflict is too great to achieve unity through deliberation alone. In many large electorates, furthermore, voters may have at best only limited and indirect control over the alternatives or candidates from which they must choose. I seek to determine voting procedures that select candidates that have wide appeal or acceptance in such an electorate.

Chapter 1 defines the voting procedures to be discussed and introduces several criteria by which they may be assessed. Chapters 2 through 4 deal with two indices of efficiency that measure (1) the tendency of each voting system to choose the Condorcet candidate—the candidate (if one exists) who can defeat all others in separate, pairwise contests—and (2) the tendency to select a candidate who enjoys high intensity of support. The methodology of computer simulation is used and is based on a variety of assumptions about the preferences of the electorate.

Chapters 5 through 9 deal with the problem of the manipulation of the outcome by individual voters or by a coalition of voters. Although probably the best known form of strategic voting is the desertion by voters— under the ordinary plurality voting system—of candidates deemed unlikely to win, all voting systems permit manipulation, as was shown by Gibbard (1973) and Satterthwaite (1975). Thus, the practical questions for social-choice theory to answer are the extent to which different systems encourage strategic calculations in voting, their effects on the nature and perceived legitimacy of the outcome, and their implications for political stability. Chapters 6 and 8 also contain extended analyses of empirical data from both elections and polls to compare outcomes that might have occurred had each of several alternative voting systems been used.

Any study of electoral procedures, including this one, is of necessity limited by the size of the window through which it views the political environment. No doubt the introduction of a new voting system would change that environment in many indirect ways that would ultimately bear on the voting outcome. Until alternative electoral systems are tested extensively in the real world, we can only indicate their likely virtues and vices. If this book contributes to that endeavor, it will have served its purpose.

ACKNOWLEDGMENTS

I wish particularly to thank Steven J. Brams, Jean Driscoll, William Riker, and Jack Nagel for valuable discussions, continued encouragement, and for their careful reading of the manuscript and for a number of useful comments. I am grateful to Jack Nagel for permission to use in this book material and ideas from a jointly authored paper. I appreciate the efforts of the reviewers, Richard Niemi and Philip Straffin, and thank them for their helpful suggestions. Sanford Thatcher of Princeton University Press is thanked for shepherding this work from manuscript to book, Cynthia Halpern for copyediting, and Andrew Mytelka for suggesting the title. Special appreciation is extended to my father Samuel Merrill, my wife Susan, and my son Andrew for reading the manuscript and making helpful comments. To them and to my daughter Amy I express appreciation for patience and support.

The data for the CPS 1972 American National Election Study used in chapters 6 and 8 was made available by the Interuniversity Consortium for Political Research and is gratefully acknowledged.

Making Multicandidate Elections
More Democratic

1

· · · · · · · · · · · · · · · · · · · ·

MULTICANDIDATE ELECTIONS:

CHOOSING A WINNER

1.1. INTRODUCTION

The votes for U.S. House majority leader by the 1976 Democratic caucus had been counted. Representative Jim Wright—to the surprise of many, perhaps to Wright himself—had cleared the last hurdle by the barest of margins to become, as it turned out, the new majority leader for the next decade and eventually the speaker of the House of Representatives.

The electoral process by which Wright wound his way to leadership says much about the effect of rules on the outcome of elections. In the United States, the top congressional leaders are chosen by a procedure almost unique in U.S. politics—although it is a variant of the method in general use in Ireland and Australia. When faced with more than two candidates, a congressional caucus conducts a series of ballots, eliminating on each ballot the candidate receiving the fewest votes.

In 1976 four Democrats—Philip Burton, Richard Bolling, John McFall, and Jim Wright—contended for majority leader. Most observers[1] place them ideologically from left to right in that order. McFall, plagued by possible scandal, withdrew after the first ballot (see table 1.1). Wright, although initially third, moved into second place on the next ballot, just in time to save himself from elimination. In the final showdown, he faced Burton, who had easily led the first two ballots. This third ballot, between the most conservative and the most liberal of the four, was the closest contest of all—Wright won by a single vote.

The outcome of the election—and the ideological stance it signalled—was highly dependent on the electoral procedure. If, as in most American elections, a single ballot had been used instead of a succession of ballots, the plurality leader, Burton, would have been elected. Had a traditional

---

[1] See Oppenheimer and Peabody (1977) for a detailed analysis of the U.S. House majority leadership race and its political background.

3

TABLE 1.1. Balloting in the 1976 U.S. House Majority Leader Race

Ballot	Burton	Bolling	McFall	Wright
First	106	81	31	77
Second	107	93	—	95
Third	147	—	—	148

runoff been stipulated, both McFall and Wright would have been eliminated on the first ballot, pitting the popular, moderate Bolling against the strongly liberal and acerbic Burton—a race most observers believe Bolling would have won (see Oppenheimer and Peabody 1977).

In fact it appears that Bolling would likely have won under all of the other alternative electoral procedures that will be introduced later in this chapter. Furthermore, he probably could have defeated each of the others in two-way races. The sensitivity, in general, of multicandidate electoral outcomes to the rules of balloting and to the decision rules that determine the winner suggests the need for a careful study of alternative procedures.

Since the late eighteenth century, a variety of procedures have been proposed to select a winner in a multicandidate election, that is, one in which there are more than two candidates. Many of these methods are known today by the names of their proposers: Borda (1781), Hare (1859), Coombs (1954), and Black (1958). Some are old and commonly used (such as the ordinary plurality and Hare systems), whereas others (such as approval voting) have only recently come to the attention of political scientists and politicians.

I will be concerned here with the design of such procedures in order to meet the political objectives of legitimacy and mandate, resistance to manipulation, simplicity, and stability. These criteria will be discussed in detail in the remainder of this chapter. The treatment in this book will be limited to elections in which a single winner is to be chosen.

1.2. LEGITIMACY AND MANDATE

An electoral system should be designed, it would seem, to select a candidate who possesses broad support from the electorate. In the 1970 presidential election in Chile, Salvadore Allende, representing the political left, received 36 percent of the popular vote; conservative Jorge Alessandri, 35 percent; while the centrist candidate, Radomiro Tomic Romero, squeezed from both sides, obtained 28 percent. Although the Chilean constitution provided that the outcome be resolved by the vote of a joint session of the Chamber of Deputies and the Senate (which eventually elected Allende), the obvious indeterminacy of the popular vote may have helped undermine Allende's mandate to govern. At the same time, the capacity of the two more extreme candidates to squeeze the centrist raises the question: would other voting systems have had the same effect?

Reaching farther back into history, we note that Abraham Lincoln won the U.S. presidency in 1860 with only 40 percent of the popular vote among four serious candidates. The others were Stephen A. Douglas (29 percent), John C. Breckinridge (18 percent), and John Bell (13 percent). Yet at least one analyst (Riker 1982a, section 9.e) estimates that Bell— who received the fewest votes—may have been acceptable to as many or more voters as Lincoln and possibly may have been acceptable to as many as any of the other candidates. Riker also believes that a majority preferred Douglas to Lincoln. Regardless of Lincoln's eventual contributions to the nation, one may ask whether his election with less than a majority mandate hastened the polarization of the nation.

In the United States, many multicandidate races occur in primaries intended to choose a party nominee. Unified support from within one's party is often necessary for success in the general election. The fates of Barry Goldwater in 1964 and George McGovern in 1972 are well known. Each won his party's nomination for president based on the fervent support of a fraction of his party's adherents, but, lacking a broad base, met disaster in the general election in November.[2]

Even if a party nominee is elected, a strong mandate grounded in wide support may be needed for the eventual winner to serve as an effective executive or legislator. The three-cornered 1983 Democratic party primary for mayor of Chicago, for example, nominated Harold Washington (with 36 percent of the vote) over Jane Byrne (34 percent) and Richard M. Daley (30 percent). Washington's subsequent close shave in the general election—in a city overwhelmingly Democratic—and his chaotic first administration beset with opposition at every turn cast serious doubt on his mandate to govern. These administrative difficulties stem in part, I would argue, from the electoral process by which Washington became mayor. Most black mayors, such as Tom Bradley in Los Angeles, Wilson Goode in Philadelphia, Andrew Young in Atlanta, and Coleman Young in De-

---

[2] See Brams and Fishburn (1983), but also Rosenstone (1983) for a contrary conclusion. The Goldwater nomination was also, in part, dependent on delegates won in caucuses, which included a disproportionate number of activists, relative to the general electorate. It has, furthermore, been argued that Goldwater may have been the strongest candidate, at least in the South, against John Kennedy and may have retained support accrued before the latter's assassination.

troit, received significant support from both whites and blacks. Washington's votes in 1983, in contrast, were largely limited to a racial minority—sufficient to eke out a plurality in a multicandidate primary but apparently not representative of broad acceptance by the electorate. Running for a second term in 1987, Washington attained majority support, receiving 53 percent of the vote in both the Democratic primary and the general election.

These examples of minority winners and others to be considered later suggest that alternative voting systems should be sought that might be more likely to lead to majority choices when broad support and a legitimizing mandate are deemed desirable. This would appear particularly apropos for executive offices (president, governor, or mayor) in which a single individual is entrusted with the power to govern.[3]

But how can one measure the tendency for an electoral system to choose a candidate with a broad support or mandate? Since the time of Condorcet (1785), perhaps the most widely accepted principle has been that if there is a candidate who can beat each of the others in a two-way race, that candidate should be selected. That such a candidate, called the Condorcet candidate, should be elected is but a natural extension of the concept of majority rule from a two-candidate to a multicandidate setting.

Before evaluating the tendency of multicandidate voting systems to choose the Condorcet candidate, one may ask the question: should all conceivable candidates who might be selected by society be considered or only those official candidates for whom actual voting takes place? How are such candidates preselected for formal voting?

The latter question is addressed in depth in Riker's (1982a) assessment of the populist and Madisonian (liberal) interpretations of the meaning of voting. Under the populist interpretation, the outcome of voting is the articulation of the collective will of the people. By contrast, the Madisonian interpretation requires only that elections permit the electorate to reject unpopular leaders. Riker argues that the disequilibrium that results from the lack of a Condorcet candidate—interpreted as one position preferred to all conceivable other alternatives—and the possibility of manipulation undercut the notion that the voting result could represent the will of the electorate (or even a majority thereof). The Madisonian ideal, however—by making no such specific demands—can still be met.

But here, in assessing the meaning and legitimacy of a voting outcome,

[3] In elections to multimember bodies (such as legislatures), representation by minority parties or factions may be desirable. Although ordinary plurality voting in single-member districts may at times provide inadvertent opportunities for such minority representation, alternative, more systematic procedures to achieve this end, such as those ensuring proportional representation, would seem to be more effective for that purpose.

I will restrict my attention to only those candidates who are formally recognized as such. I will discuss, however, the question of the effects of voting procedures on the opportunities for new candidates to enter a race effectively and whether each system favors the entry of candidates with centrist or extremist positions.

The Condorcet criterion ignores the question of intensity of support. If we interpret a voter's evaluation of a candidate as a utility[4] we may assess the aggregate intensity of support by computing the social or average utility over all voters (see, e.g., Harsanyi 1977) and argue that the candidate who on the average is rated most highly by the voters should be elected. As we shall see, this criterion and that of Condorcet need not agree.

1.3. Resistance to Manipulation

Manipulation by *insincere voting*[5] (i.e., voting in a way that does not reflect one's true preference order) or by other strategies, to be introduced later, can significantly alter the outcome. Such manipulation may perniciously undermine the selection of the candidate with the strongest support and call into question the legitimacy of the winner.

In other situations, however, this kind of manipulation may have just the opposite effect, permitting the selection of a Condorcet candidate who would otherwise have been defeated. As we will see in chapter 6, not only the opportunities for manipulation but also its likely consequences vary greatly from one voting procedure to another.

The best-known form of insincere voting occurs under ordinary plurality voting when a voter deserts a first choice who is perceived as unlikely to win and supports instead one of the front-runners who is less preferred. Many voters may be torn between supporting their favorite and making their vote count by voting for a front-runner, being unable to register both feelings. One may therefore seek a voting system that only infrequently presents voters with such dilemmas. Such strategic voting, when it involves deserting minor party candidates to avoid "wasting votes," may, however, strengthen a two-party system at the same time that it poses dilemmas for the individual voter (see section 4 below).

[4] A voter's utility for a candidate is a number intended to represent the voter's valuation of the candidate. Operationally, if a voter is asked to rate candidates on a scale of, say, zero to ten, her ratings may be interpreted as utilities.

[5] The term *insincere voting* is commonly used in social-choice theory to refer to any expressed preference that differs from one's true preference. Such an action might be taken for strategic purposes. Despite the pejorative connotations of the word insincere in ordinary usage, no such meaning is intended here. Although the term will be used throughout the book, the implications of insincere voting will receive special attention in chapters 6 and 7.

In devising alternative procedures, one must be careful not to complicate unduly the job of the electorate. The simplicity of the balloting method helps ensure that voters are capable of voting as they intend with a minimum of mistakes. Relative freedom from opportunities to manipulate the outcome by misrepresenting preferences is one factor that helps in achieving simplicity and fairness to voters. Simplicity of the decision rule aids public understanding and acceptance of the outcome, and thus, the legitimacy of the process.

1.4. POLITICAL STABILITY

Each of the foregoing criteria impinges on the capacity of a voting system to promote political stability. Of signal importance is the acceptance of the winner as legitimate by the electorate—both in the sense of having achieved an adequate mandate and the relative freedom of the process from manipulation. The belief that a loser is preferred by a majority of the electorate to the winner or enjoys greater intensity of support can call into question that legitimacy. These two criteria may be at odds with one another. Lincoln, for example, enjoyed great intensity of support in the 1860 U.S. presidential election, while the broader, but less intense, support for Douglas and Bell suggests that one or both may have been preferred by majorities over Lincoln.

The differential impact of multicandidate voting systems on the electoral outcome, illustrated earlier in this chapter, is well known (see, e.g., Rae 1971, Straffin 1980, Riker 1982a, Bogdanor and Butler 1983). The influence of the electoral system in use on the number and nature of political parties, factions, or candidacies may also have a profound effect on political stability (see Duverger 1963, 1984, Riker 1982b, Miller 1983).

Duverger formulated as a law a principle that had been discussed by numerous writers before him, namely, that ordinary plurality voting favors a two-party system. Although Canada and India are exceptions to this claim, there appears to be considerable empirical support (in the United States and Britain) for the argument that a plurality election without a runoff provides incentives for voters to focus on two candidates and for factions or parties to coalesce in an effort to receive a plurality of the votes on the single ballot. A runoff, by contrast, permits losing factions or parties a second chance in which they may bargain with one of the two leaders in return for their endorsement. The anticipation of this opportunity may encourage greater factionalism or proliferation of parties before the first ballot. In preparation for the second ballot, however, this opportunity promotes coalition building.

Canon (1978) studied the relationship of voting procedures to factionalism in the Democratic gubernatorial primaries in sixteen southern and border states of the United States during 1932 to 1977. Using a reasonable index of factionalism, he found this value lower in all but one of the six states using ordinary plurality than in the ten states employing a runoff. Thus Canon's findings tend to support the Duverger hypothesis. As Riker (1983b) points out, the Canadian and Indian exceptions may be accounted for by restricting the hypothesis. For a decentralized government such as that of Canada, different pairs of parties may be prominent in different provinces, giving rise to a multiparty system nationally. In a nation in which one centrist party (like the Congress party in India) maintains a prolonged domination of the government over smaller parties to the left and right, these latter parties may be unable to coalesce for ideological reasons.

Much of Duverger's argument contrasts ordinary plurality voting with proportional representation in multimember districts. This part of his work is not directly relevant to the concerns of the present book, which focuses on single-winner elections. There appears to be little evidence, either theoretical or empirical, concerning the impact of single-winner voting systems, other than ordinary plurality or runoff, on the possible proliferation of factions or parties. One should be careful, however, not to infer that alternative single-winner voting procedures would promote factionalism simply because they are different from ordinary plurality or because their multiwinner counterparts may have been shown to have this effect.

1.5. Arrow's Impossibility Result and Its Implications

Were it possible to design a multicandidate voting system satisfying all desirable political objectives, the choice of such a system would be simple and there would be no reason for this book. Remarkably, even a seemingly modest list of criteria may be self-contradictory, that is the satisfaction of one criterion may be incompatible with the satisfaction of others.

Arrow (1951) showed that no multicandidate system based on transitive[6] rankings by voters can simultaneously satisfy the following

[6] A voter's preference order is said to be *transitive*, if, whenever the voter prefers A over B and B over C, she also prefers A over C. One of the major findings of social-choice theory, the *paradox of voting*, first observed by Condorcet, is that a transitive ordering for all voters does not ensure that the social ordering will be transitive. For example, suppose there are three candidates A, B, and C, and three voters, with respective preference orders ABC, BCA, and CAB. Then A is preferred over B by two voters to one. Similarly, B is preferred over C and C over A, in each case by two votes to one. Each of the three candidates beats one of the

CHAPTER 1

four conditions: monotonicity, independence of irrelevant alternatives, nonimposition, and nondictatorship. As Arrow's axioms have been extensively analyzed elsewhere (see, e.g., Kelly 1978), I will only describe each intuitively here.

Roughly speaking, a voting system violates *monotonicity* if a candidate can achieve a win because of loss of support (or fail to win because of a gain in support). A system is *independent of irrelevant alternatives* if the relative standings of the candidates cannot be altered by the entry of additional candidates into the race. *Nonimposition* means that the outcome cannot be imposed independently of the voters' preferences, that is no candidate loses to another for every possible voting outcome. *Nondictatorship* means that the result need not always coincide with the preferences of one particular voter.

Arrow's impossibility theorem shows that any multicandidate voting system based on transitive rankings will violate one or more of these basic expectations at least some of the time. Accordingly, we must evaluate the degree to which these and other desired criteria are met.

Much work in social-choice theory—in assessing electoral procedures—has focused on which procedures logically satisfy political desiderata such as monotonicity or the Condorcet criterion. Under this approach, the question is: does the procedure satisfy the criterion in all conceivable circumstances? The construction of a single counterexample is sufficient to prove a violation of such a criterion. This kind of study, although theoretically elegant, is limited in the sense that it offers us no information about the likelihood of such a violation taking place in practice.

By contrast, I assume that the legitimacy of an electoral outcome does not require the logical certainty of a given political desideratum, but only its likelihood. This likelihood will be assessed for a number of electoral procedures. Inferences will be drawn from (1) theoretical models, (2) computer simulations, and (3) empirical data involving elections and polls.

The logical possibility of a violation of a desired condition may, at times, induce political manipulation by voters, candidates, or parties to exploit such a loophole. The satisfaction of a political desiderata with high probability, nevertheless, appears to satisfy Riker's expectation under the Madisonian interpretation of voting, for the mere likelihood that offensive behavior by an incumbent will be met by electoral rejection is sufficient—in Riker's view—to meet the Madisonian ideal (Riker 1982a, 243).

---

others, but each is also beaten by some other candidate. In social-choice terminology, there is, hence, no Condorcet candidate, because each candidate can be beaten by at least one other in pairwise contests.

10

I will concentrate on the following criteria, which lend themselves to the methodologies described above, for judging multicandidate electoral systems:

a. To what extent does the system tend to choose the Condorcet candidate, if one exists?
b. To what extent does the system select a candidate of high intensity of support?
c. Does the system encourage insincere voting? If so, what are the effects on the outcome?
d. Does the system permit voting strategies that would not be optimal for the voter under any circumstances?
e. Which of Arrow's conditions are satisfied, and to what extent?
f. Does the system tend to choose centrist or extremist candidates?
g. Does the system encourage the proliferation of candidates?

1.6. Multicandidate Electoral Systems

Seven electoral systems—intended to serve as representatives of the major types—will be studied, although the methodologies are not limited to these. It will be important in describing voting systems to distinguish between the *balloting method* (which specifies how the voter is permitted to cast her votes, e.g., a single vote, several votes, or a ranking of candidates) and the *decision rule* (which specifies how the ballots are to be aggregated to determine the winner). A *voting system* is a combination of these two components and may be designated, when precision is necessary, by two words (or phrases or abbreviations), the first indicating the balloting method and the second, the decision rule.

Classifying by decision rule, we will consider three major types of voting systems: three plurality systems (single-vote plurality, approval voting, and the Borda count), three elimination procedures (the Hare, single-vote plurality with runoff, and Coombs systems), and one Condorcet completion method (Black). This list includes three single-winner electoral systems currently in use in English-speaking countries (single-vote plurality, runoff, and Hare).

Plurality is a decision rule: the candidate with the greatest number of votes wins, without regard to thresholds. A particular plurality system is characterized by its balloting method, which specifies the number of votes the voter may cast for each of the various candidates. Such constraints apply symmetrically to all voters and candidates. The following three plurality systems will be considered here:

1. *Single-vote plurality.* The balloting method permits each voter to cast one vote for exactly one candidate. This system, heretofore called ordinary plurality, is in general use in the United States, Canada, and Britain.

2. *Approval plurality (approval voting).* The approval ballot permits each voter to cast a vote for (i.e., to "approve") one, two, three, . . . or any number of candidates (but to cast only one vote per candidate). Equivalently, each voter says "yes" or "no" (to approve or disapprove) for each candidate. The decision rule is plurality: the candidate approved of by the most voters wins. For simplicity, this system will be referred to as approval voting, except in chapter 7 where approval balloting is combined with each of several decision rules.[7]

Under this system, unlike single-vote plurality, a voter who favors a candidate unlikely to win can vote both for her and for one of the front-runners. For example, under approval voting, supporters of Jesse Jackson in the 1984 Democratic presidential primaries could vote for both Jackson and also, say, Walter Mondale. Apparently proposed only during the last decade, approval voting has come under intensive study in the last few years (see Brams 1976, 1978, 1987; Brams and Fishburn 1978, 1983; Carter 1987; Fishburn and Brams 1981a, b; Hoffman 1982; Kellett and Mott 1977; Kiewiet 1979; Merrill 1979; Merrill and Nagel 1987; Morin 1980; Nagel 1987; Niemi 1984; and Weber, 1977).

3. *Borda count.* Proposed by Jean-Charles de Borda (1781), the ballot requires each voter to rank the candidates. For K candidates, the voter is permitted to cast K-1 votes for one candidate (e.g., a first choice), K-2 votes for a second candidate, down to 0 votes for the last candidate. Effectively, the plurality decision rule of the Borda count chooses that candidate who is, on the average, ranked highest by the voters. The Borda system is used today to obtain collective rankings, such as rankings of collegiate football teams by sportswriters. Studies of the Borda count have been made by Black (1976), Chamberlin and Courant (1983), Ludwin (1978), and Young (1975).

THE NEXT three systems are *elimination* procedures. Although each involves plurality calculations, its decision rule is not based solely on the summation of scores. The systems are:

[7] For three candidates, approval voting is equivalent to *negative voting* (see Brams 1976) under which the voter may cast one positive vote for a single candidate (equivalent to voting only for that candidate under approval voting) or cast one negative vote for a single candidate (equivalent to voting for both the other two candidates under approval voting). For more than three candidates, approval voting offers more options than negative voting. Under negative voting, the voter cannot cast both a positive and a negative vote; to do so, however, would be equivalent to the Borda count for three candidates.

4. *Hare.* The Hare or *single-transferable-vote* system is used for single-winner races to elect members of the Australian House of Representatives,[8] where it is also called preferential or alternative voting. A ballot providing a complete preference ordering is obtained from each voter. If no candidate obtains a majority of first-place votes, the decision rule specifies that the candidate with the fewest first-place votes is eliminated, and the second-place votes of her supporters are transferred to augment the first-place totals of the remaining candidates. This process is repeated until one candidate has a majority and is declared the winner.

A *successive-elimination* contest, in which the lowest vote-getter is eliminated on each of a succession of ballots, is structurally identical to the Hare system, provided that voters do not alter their reported preference ordering (for example, for strategic reasons) between ballots. Successive elimination ballots are used by the respective party caucuses to select the majority leaders of the U.S. Senate and House of Representatives.

For recent research on the Hare method, see Doron and Kronick (1977), Fishburn (1982), and Fishburn and Brams (1983). Experience with its use in Australia is described by Penniman (1977) and in multi-member districts in Ireland by O'Leary (1979) and Bogdanor and Butler (1983). Analysis of the use of successive-elimination ballots is reported in Brams and Fishburn (1981) and with further background in Oppenheimer and Peabody (1977).

5. *Single-vote plurality with runoff.* The runoff system is used in a number of primary elections in the United States, especially in the southern states, and in the presidential elections of the French Fifth Republic. The runoff procedure augments single-vote plurality. If no candidate receives a majority[9] on the first ballot, a second ballot is held to choose between the top two vote-getters. The method can also be viewed as a modification of the Hare elimination procedure in which all but the top two candidates (receiving the most first-place votes) are eliminated at once. It is equivalent to successive eliminations when the number of candidates is three.

6. *Coombs.* A second modification of the Hare system, suggested by the psychologist Clyde Coombs (1954), is obtained by successively eliminat-

[8] The Hare system is also used in multimember districts (as in Ireland and the Australian Senate), wherein it implements proportional representation by tending to elect members to seats roughly in proportion to the popular support for each party.

[9] In some cases, such as party runoffs in New York City, 40 percent of the vote is required to avoid a second ballot instead of a majority. French parliamentary (as opposed to presidential) elections in the Fifth Republic have used a modified runoff requiring that a party meet a threshold (usually 12.5 percent of the registered voters) to reach the second ballot. Such a procedure permits more than two candidates on the second ballot, but it tends to encourage the formation of coalitions between parties or candidates.

ing the candidate with the most last-place votes. Insofar as voters wish to vote against unacceptable candidates, as opposed to voting for preferred candidates, this system is intended to eliminate unacceptable candidates.

THE LAST procedure is a *Condorcet completion* method, that is, a method that selects the Condorcet candidate if such a candidate exists. The ballot requires a complete preference ordering. The principal such procedure considered in this book is that of Black.

7. *Black*. Under Duncan Black's proposal (D. Black 1958), the Condorcet candidate is chosen, if one exists; if not, the Borda rule is used. Black's rationale for the choice of the Borda rule is that the Borda score for each candidate is the sum of the votes this candidate would get if placed against each other candidate in turn.[10] Thus Black's completion rule can be interpreted as a quantitative version of a completion method devised by Copeland (see chapter 3, note 5) which specifies as the winner the candidate who would win the most pairwise contests. Yet another completion rule, that of Dodgson (see section 6.5), awards victory to the candidate whose maximum pairwise loss to an opponent is the smallest.

---

[10] This alternative interpretation of the Borda count is derived as follows. The Borda score given by each voter to a candidate is the number of other candidates who are less preferred than that candidate. Summed over all voters, this score amounts to the total number of preferences for this candidate over others.

2

....

CONDORCET EFFICIENCY

2.1. INTRODUCTION

No criterion for evaluating a multicandidate voting procedure appears more pervasive than Condorcet's. This criterion, as we have seen, requires that if there is a candidate who can defeat each of the others in pairwise contests (i.e., is preferred by a majority to each), that candidate should be chosen as the winner. Such a candidate, when one exists, is known as the Condorcet candidate.

For example, suppose there are three candidates A, B, and C, and seven voters with preference orders as shown.

2 voters	3 voters	2 voters
A	C	B
B	A	A
C	B	C

Since A is preferred to B by five voters to two, and is preferred to C four to three, A is the Condorcet candidate, despite the fact that A does not have a plurality of first-place votes.

With the obvious exception of Condorcet completion methods, such as the one suggested by Black, none of the voting systems introduced in chapter 1 guarantees the selection of a Condorcet candidate, even if there is one. Hence we must compare the degree to which these various systems meet that standard. As we will see, there are significant differences among these voting systems.

For each voting system, *Condorcet efficiency* is defined to be the percentage of a given class of elections for which the Condorcet candidate is chosen, provided there is one. For example, if we consider one hundred elections in which a Condorcet candidate exists, and we find that a certain electoral system selects the Condorcet candidate in eighty-five of them, we say its Condorcet efficiency is 85 percent.

15

In order to compute Condorcet efficiency, the class of elections to be studied must be specified. Since information about voter preferences sufficient to determine Condorcet candidates in historical elections is sparse, many researchers have turned to the power of the computer to simulate elections by Monte Carlo techniques.

Such techniques use random numbers—generated by computer—to represent utilities or positions of voters and candidates. These utilities and positions are not intended to reflect the behavior of specific individuals. Rather, the distribution of these values taken in aggregate can, by careful control of the generation process, accurately model the behavior of an electorate or a field of candidates.

In order to generate voter utilities and preferences, I will consider two models: a random-society model and a spatial model of electoral competition. Following a brief description of these models, I will provide justification for their use in representing voter behavior.

To generate a *random society*, for each voter, candidate utilities are chosen as independent, uniformly distributed random variates on a common interval from 0 to 1 (see, e.g., Weber 1977). With the exception of approval voting,[1] voter utilities are used (in the computation of Condorcet efficiency) only to determine preference orders, that is, a voter is assumed to prefer candidate A to candidate B if his utility for A exceeds that for B. Because the utilities are independent and uniformly distributed, a random society is an *impartial culture* (see, e.g., Fishburn and Gehrlein 1976 and 1977), in which all preference orders are assumed equally likely.

Spatial models, originally developed in the field of economics (see, e.g., Hotelling 1929), were first used to represent electoral competitions by Downs (1957) and have been studied extensively during the past decade.[2] Under a *spatial model* both voters and candidates are assumed to be placed in space (either uni- or multidimensional) according to the positions they take or prefer on certain issues or according to personal characteristics, each of which corresponds to a dimension (see figure 2.1). (For simplicity, we will use the term "issue" to refer either to an issue or to a personal characteristic.) Thus an actor's position on issue 1 is represented

---

[1] For approval voting, voters are assumed to use optimal strategies in the sense of maximizing expected utility for equiprobable outcomes, i.e., to cast votes for all candidates whose utilities exceed the mean over all candidates for that voter (see chapter 5). In the current chapter, all voting is assumed to be sincere. Condorcet efficiency for insincere voting will be investigated in chapter 6.

[2] See, e.g., Davis, Hinich, and Ordeshook (1970); Aldrich (1975, 1977); Riker and Ordeshook (1973); McKelvey 1975; Aldrich and McKelvey (1977); Hinich and Pollard (1980); Enelow and Hinich (1981, 1984); and Poole and Rosenthal (1984).

by the distance of his ideal point to the left or right of the vertical axis; his position on issue 2, by the distance up or down from the horizontal axis, etc. In such a rational-choice model, the ideal point associated with a voter represents the point of maximum preference or utility.

The simulations in this and the following chapter are taken from Merrill (1984). It is assumed that a voter's utility for a candidate decreases linearly with (Euclidean) distance d between the voter's ideal point and the position of the candidate (see, however, chapter 4 for the effect of a non-linear utility function). For example, in figure 2.1, the voter V would have preference order ACBD, determined by distance from the ideal point V. I assume further that the preference order for each voter is determined by the voter's utility function.

Both voters and candidates will be generated in the simulations from multivariate normal distributions (see the Glossary for the definitions of this and other technical terms). Thus, the scatter of voters (or candidates) will be mound-shaped, with the greatest concentration in the center. In addition to the number of candidates, the number of dimensions, the correlation matrix representing interrelationships among issues in the spatial model, and the relative dispersion of candidates and voters will be varied. As in the case of the random-society model, utilities are used only to determine preference orders, except for approval voting, where the expected utility is used to determine optimal strategies, as before.[3]

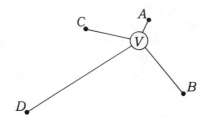

FIGURE 2.1. Example of Two-dimensional Spatial Model.

---

[3] Fishburn and Gehrlein (1976 and 1977) conducted simulations for Condorcet efficiency for single-vote plurality, single-vote plurality with runoff, and methods like approval voting (with and without a runoff). They considered a variety of distributions of voter profiles (including impartial and partial cultures) but did not use a spatial model approach. Nevertheless, the spatial model simulation results described here appear to agree with theirs insofar as they are comparable. Fishburn and Gehrlein's results indicate a high Condorcet efficiency for approval voting with runoff. However, as Fishburn himself points out in a paper with Brams (1981), such a system could be manipulated (see also chapter 7 below). The first simulations for Condorcet efficiency under spatial model assumptions were performed by

The simulation results for Condorcet efficiency, to be described in detail in section 2.2, demonstrate significant differences among voting systems but a remarkable similarity between the spatial and random-society models. Although Condorcet efficiency drops as the number of candidates increases and rises as the number of spatial dimensions grows larger, these effects are rather uniform over these electoral procedures.

The highest efficiencies occur, in general, for the Coombs and Borda procedures, and, of course, for any Condorcet completion method, such as that of Black. These are followed by the Hare, runoff, and approval voting methods, usually in that order. The single-vote plurality method—the most commonly used system in English-speaking countries—has a significantly lower Condorcet efficiency than any of the others.

Unless voting is compulsory, not all eligible citizens are voters. This fact bears on the spatial analysis of voting behavior only to the extent that abstention is related to the relative positions of candidates and voters in the spatial model. Riker and Ordeshook (1973) suggest two reasons for abstention that are both dependent on spatial parameters. Abstention due to indifference is assumed to be more likely when two (major) candidates are about the same spatial distance from the voter. Abstention due to alienation is assumed to be high when no candidate is near the voter.

If the effect of indifference is significant, one would expect that voters who are equidistant from the two main candidates would be more likely than others to be indifferent. Likewise, in the case of alienation, we would expect voters at great distances from either candidate to be more likely than others not to vote. The spatial plots of voters and nonvoters by Poole and Rosenthal (1984) for the 1968 and 1976 presidential elections, however, suggest no support for these expectations. This suggests that there may be no significant loss of realism by making no special provisions for abstention in my simulations.

Campbell, Converse, Miller, and Stokes, in their classic empirical study (1960), suggested that in the 1950s there was little or no underlying structure to the public's attitudes on separate issue questions. Such a conclusion gives support to a random society as a model for voter behavior.

More recently, evidence to the contrary has been mounting. Niemi and Weisberg (1976, 79) state that "Alternative definitions and measurements

---

Chamberlin and Cohen (1978). Nurmi (1986) conducted simulations for the likelihood that a voting system would choose the *Condorcet loser* (i.e., a candidate who could be beaten by each other candidate in two-way races), if such a candidate exists. For a large electorate and both impartial and dual cultures (see Glossary) he found this undesirable likelihood substantial and greater for single-vote plurality than for approval voting, at least for four or more candidates.

suggest that the thinking of the American electorate is now, and perhaps was even in the 1950's, much more ideological than we had begun to believe." The studies of Nie and Andersen (1976) and Aldrich (1980), among others, support this view. Based on data from a CBS/New York Times poll, Aldrich (1980, 164–65) argues that citizens tend to support candidates whose policies are most like their own—that is, they tend to prefer candidates whose positions in a spatial model are nearer their own.

Chamberlin and Featherston (1986) analyzed the distribution of preference orders for voters in two types of real elections: the election of presidents of the American Psychological Association and "thermometer" ratings based on survey data collected by the National Election Studies concerning potential U.S. presidential candidates. They employed two indices: (1) the Gini index, which measures the uniformity or equity with which different preference orders were expressed by voters, and (2) a normalized Kemeny index, which measures the average distance (distance is defined as the number of adjacent pairwise switches needed to convert one preference order to another) between each voter-preference order and the winning order. They found the values for the Gini and Kemeny indices for these real elections to be intermediate between those for impartial-culture and spatial models.

Although the more recent analyses appear to suggest that the spatial model is a more realistic representation of voting behavior, it appears that electoral behavior possesses both random and spatial components. Accordingly, simulations based on each of these models may shed light on the effects of different electoral systems.

2.2. SIMULATION RESULTS
FOR CONDORCET EFFICIENCY

Simulated Condorcet efficiencies are presented in table 2.1 and figure 2.2 for a random society for $n = 25$ voters and candidate fields of size $K = 2$, 3, 4, 5, 7, and 10.[4] For three candidates, the elimination methods and of

---

[4] For each candidate field, 10,000 elections (each involving 25 voters) were simulated, except for $K = 7$ (5,000 elections) and $K = 10$ (2,500 elections). The standard errors for the estimates range from about 0.4 percentage points to double that value for $K = 10$. (The standard error of an estimate is defined as the standard deviation of all estimates based on repeated sampling for a given sample size.) Simulations for a larger number of voters (201) but fewer elections (1,000) suggest that Condorcet efficiency for a random-society model is not very sensitive to the number of voters. Increasing the number of voters decreases the Condorcet efficiency slightly in nearly every case (up to 7 percentage points for single-vote

CHAPTER 2

TABLE 2.1. Condorcet Efficiencies for a Random Society (25 voters)

Voting system	Number of candidates					
	2	3	4	5	7	10
Single-vote plurality	100.0	79.1	69.4	62.1	52.0	42.6
Runoff	100.0	96.2	90.1	83.6	73.5	61.3
Hare	100.0	96.2	92.7	89.1	84.8	77.9
Approval	100.0	76.0	69.8	67.1	63.7	61.3
Borda	100.0	90.8	87.3	86.2	85.3	84.3
Coombs	100.0	96.3	93.4	90.2	86.1	81.1
Black	100.0	100.0	100.0	100.0	100.0	100.0
Social-utility maximizer[a]	100.0	84.4	80.2	77.9	77.2	77.8
% Condorcet winners[b]	100.0	91.6	83.4	75.8	64.3	52.5

SOURCE: S. Merrill, "A Comparison of Efficiency of Multicandidate Electoral Systems," *American Journal of Political Science* 28 (1984): 28, Table 1; reprinted with permission.
[a] See chapter 3.
[b] Percent of elections for which a Condorcet candidate exists.

course Black's procedure are the most likely to choose the Condorcet candidate. As the number of candidates increases, the Borda count and approval voting methods improve relative to the elimination methods. Single-vote plurality is almost uniformly the weakest performer. Also indicated in table 2.1 is the percentage of elections in which Condorcet candidates exist in the simulation (see, e.g., Gehrlein 1983, for the exact values) and the Condorcet efficiency of the candidate highest in social utility (see chapter 3).

To estimate Condorcet efficiency under spatial model assumptions, over forty simulations with a variety of patterns of parameter levels were performed. The number of candidates ranged over 3, 4, 5, and 7; the number of spatial dimensions was varied from 1 to 4.[5] Various correlation ma-

plurality with seven candidates), but it alters the ranking of the voting systems in only one (statistically insignificant) case.

[5] Each simulation run under spatial model assumptions employed 200 replicates of candidate fields, each replicate being combined with each of five simulated electorates of 201

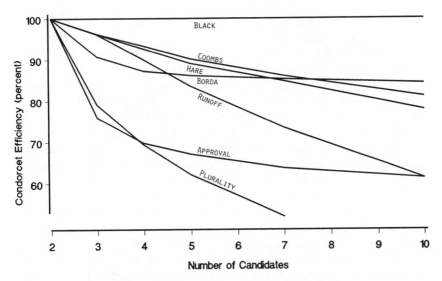

FIGURE 2.2. Condorcet Efficiency for a Random Society (25 Voters).
SOURCE: S. Merrill, "A Comparison of Efficiency of Multicandidate Electoral Systems," *American Journal of Political Science* 28 (1984): 29, Figure 1; reprinted with permission.

trices were employed, including the one investigated by Chamberlin and Cohen (1978). The number of voters (201) in each run was selected to represent a mass electorate.[6]

For both voters and candidates, preferred positions in the spatial model were generated from identical (multivariate normal) distributions, except

---

voters each. This yields standard errors for Condorcet efficiency of about 2 percentage points, so that the least significant difference for pairwise comparison is about 6 percentage points at the 0.05 level. To facilitate the large number of simulations involved, in each case rotation to principal axes was employed to diagonalize the correlation matrix (Morrison 1976, ch. 8).

[6] Under spatial model assumptions, an increase in the number of voters from 25 to 500 was found to have a significant and differential effect on Condorcet efficiency for the voting systems studied: for approval voting, efficiency increases about 10 percentage points, whereas for single-vote plurality, runoff, and Hare, efficiency decreases by 0 to 15 points. Simulation with electorates of sizes ranging from 25 to 500 indicate that Condorcet efficiency levels off as the electorate size reaches 100 to 200. Hence an electorate of about 200 voters may be used to measure Condorcet efficiency for any large electorate. An odd number (201) of voters was used to avoid two-way ties and thereby to facilitate computation. This had no substantive effect on the results. In case m (> 1) candidates (including the Condorcet candidate) are tied as winners under a particular voting system for a particular election, the tie was assumed resolved by lot. Accordingly, $1/m$ elections were recorded as choosing the Condorcet candidate, which may be interpreted as an expected value.

for a scale factor representing the *relative dispersion* (RD) of candidates and voters. Specifically, the relative dispersion is the ratio of the standard deviation of the distribution of candidates and the standard deviation of the distribution of voters.[7] The values for RD used in the simulations are 0.5 and 1.0. These values reflect the approximate range of relative dispersion for a number of issue dimensions in two U.S. presidential elections, estimated and scaled by Aldrich and McKelvey (1977).[8]

A relative dispersion of 1.0 indicates that candidates and voters are equally dispersed spatially. This is depicted in figure 2.3, which presents a simulated electorate of 201 voters (dots) and 5 candidates (circles), each generated from a bivariate normal distribution with standard deviation = 1.0.[9] A relative dispersion of 0.5 indicates that the standard deviation of candidate positions is one-half that for voter positions (see figure 2.4, which is identical to figure 2.3 except that the standard deviation for candidates [but not voters] has been reduced by one-half).

Table 2.2 provides a comparison of Condorcet efficiencies under random-society and spatial-model assumptions for 201 voters and 5 candidates. Two levels are given for each of the following parameters: number of dimensions, correlation,[10] and relative dispersion. Note that when candidate and voter dispersions are the same, the spatial model results are

[7] More precisely, this ratio is the common ratio of the standard deviations of the marginal distributions for candidates and voters.

[8] The spatial analysis of issue positions in the 1968 and 1976 U.S. presidential elections performed by Poole and Rosenthal (1984) suggest that presidential candidates are more polarized than voters, i.e., that RD may be greater than 1.0. Still, voters whose responses to issue questions place them in the central mass of the electorate may simply be indifferent to ideological questions. A spatial model is largely irrelevant to such voters, whose behavior may better be represented in another way, such as by a random-society model. A spatial model can provide insight about voting behavior only for voters who make issue-oriented choices. Suppose voters reporting more extreme positions are in fact more likely than voters reporting centrist positions (or whose average responses fall in the center) to reflect ideological choices. The distribution of issue-oriented voters would then be more widely dispersed than that of the overall electorate. Thus candidates, even though they may be more dispersed than the overall electorate, might not be more spread out than the issue-oriented voters, i.e., those voters for whom a spatial model is relevant. This would suggest that the apparent high value of RD from the Poole and Rosenthal data may not be appropriate for the spatial model considered here.

[9] The correlation for this scatter plot is 0.5; the distribution has been rotated to principal axes.

[10] The correlation matrices used to produce this table assume that all off-diagonal correlations are the same (either all 0 or all 0.5). The number of dimensions and the correlation structure can be incorporated into a single parameter (which agrees with dimension for uncorrelated coordinates). Condorcet efficiency is found to be approximately linear as a function of the logarithm of this measure of generalized dimension (see chapter 4).

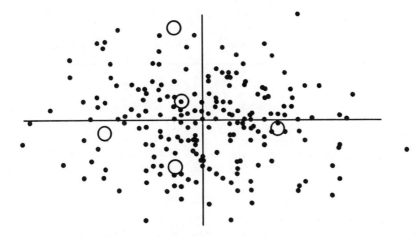

FIGURE 2.3. Simulated Scatter Plot of 201 Voters and 5 Candidates from Bivariate Normal Distributions: Relative Dispersion = 1.0.
SOURCE: S. Merrill, "A Comparison of Efficiency of Multicandidate Electoral Systems," *American Journal of Political Science* 28 (1984): 32, Figure 2.a; reprinted with permission.

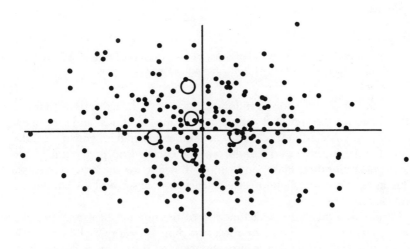

FIGURE 2.4. Simulated Scatter Plot of 201 Voters and 5 Candidates from Bivariate Normal Distributions: Relative Dispersion = 0.5.
SOURCE: S. Merrill, "A Comparison of Efficiency of Multicandidate Electoral Systems," *American Journal of Political Science* 28 (1984): 33, Figure 2.b; reprinted with permission.

TABLE 2.2. Condorcet Efficiencies under Random Society and
Spatial Model Assumptions (201 voters, 5 candidates)
C = correlation between variates; D = number of dimensions.

Voting System	Random society	Spatial model							
		Dispersion = 1.0				Dispersion = 0.5			
		$C = 0.5$		$C = 0.0$		$C = 0.5$		$C = 0.0$	
		$D = 2$	$D = 4$	$D = 2$	$D = 4$	$D = 2$	$D = 4$	$D = 2$	$D = 4$
Single-vote plurality	60	57	67	61	81	21	28	27	42
Runoff	82	80	87	79	96	31	44	39	62
Hare	88	78	86	83	97	34	50	38	72
Approval	67	74	78	81	84	73	76	75	82
Borda	85	86	89	89	92	84	87	86	88
Coombs	90	97	97	95	97	90	91	90	94
Black	100	100	100	100	100	100	100	100	100
Social-utility maximizer	78	83	88	88	90	80	85	83	86
% Condorcet winners	76	99+	99	99+	99+	98	98	98	99

SOURCE: S. Merrill, "A Comparison of Efficiency of Multicandidate Electoral Systems," *American Journal of Political Science* 28 (1984): 31, Table 2; reprinted with permission.

fairly similar to those for a random society, with the exceptions that the efficiencies for the approval voting and Coombs methods (and for the dimension 4, correlation 0 scenario) are somewhat higher. For low candidate dispersion, however, Condorcet efficiencies drop precipitously for single-vote plurality, Hare, and runoff (but not for the other systems). This latter effect for Condorcet efficiency was observed by Chamberlin and Cohen (1978).

Condorcet efficiencies as a function of the number of candidates are presented in figures 2.5 and 2.6 for a two-dimensional spatial model with correlation = 0.5, for relative dispersions of 1.0 and 0.5, respectively. The ranking of voting systems according to Condorcet efficiency is relatively insensitive to the number of dimensions and the correlation structure, so these plots can be taken as typical of the spatial models under consideration. Note that after Black, which is 100 percent Condorcet efficient by definition, Coombs is the strongest performer and single-vote plurality the weakest. The Condorcet efficiencies of Coombs, Borda, and approval voting are unperturbed as the relative dispersion of candidates to voters decreases, whereas those for Hare, runoff, and single-vote plurality plummet. In fact, for relative dispersion = 0.5 with 5 or more candidates, the last-named system is no more likely to choose the Condorcet candidate than a lottery.

Condorcet efficiency for the two elimination procedures, Coombs and Hare, are strikingly different, especially for low candidate dispersion. The explanation is straightforward. In a symmetric spatial model, the Condorcet candidate is the candidate nearest the center (for a sufficiently large n). As noted by Chamberlin and Cohen (1978), such a candidate tends to receive few last-place votes (since preference order is a function of voter-to-candidate distance). Hence, he is likely to withstand elimination under the Coombs method. However, squeezed by surrounding opponents, a centrist candidate may receive few first-place votes and be eliminated under Hare.

2.3. CONCLUSIONS

In this chapter, Condorcet efficiency has been assessed for both a random-society model and a multivariate normal spatial model (in which utility decreases linearly with distance from voter to candidate). Mixtures of the two models, in which a proportion of voters are randomly chosen from each model, yield Condorcet efficiencies intermediate between those of the two pure models. The efficiencies for the mixed models are, in general, nearer to the spatial model values than might be expected if the effect of mixing were linear. This result provides further support for preferring a spatial model, even if only a small fraction of voters behaves ideologically.

The choice, furthermore, between the spatial and random-society models appears to be less of a determinant of Condorcet efficiency than is one particular characteristic of a spatial model: namely, the relative dispersion of candidates and voters. We draw the following inferences from the simulations:

CONCLUSION 1. *As long as candidate and voter dispersion are the same, both spatial and random-society models lead, in multicandidate elections, to high Condorcet efficiency for the Black, Coombs, and Borda procedures, intermediate efficiency for the Hare, runoff, and approval voting methods, and the lowest efficiency for single-vote plurality.*

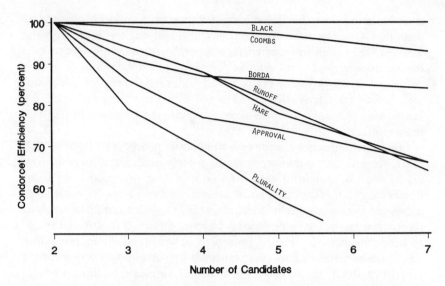

FIGURE 2.5. Condorcet Efficiency under Spatial Model Assumptions (201 Voters, 2 Dimensions, Correlation = 0.5, Relative Dispersion = 1.0).
SOURCE: S. Merrill, "A Comparison of Efficiency of Multicandidate Electoral Systems," *American Journal of Political Science* 28 (1984): 34, Figure 2.c; reprinted with permission.

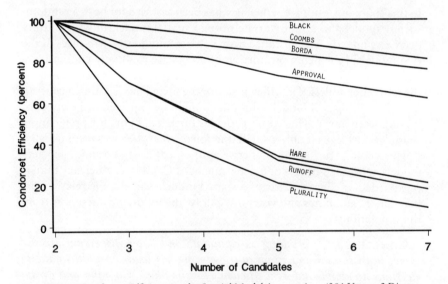

FIGURE 2.6. Condorcet Efficiency under Spatial Model Assumptions (201 Voters, 2 Dimensions, Correlation = 0.5, Relative Dispersion = 0.5).
SOURCE: S. Merrill, "A Comparison of Efficiency of Multicandidate Electoral Systems," *American Journal of Political Science* 28 (1984): 35, Figure 2.d; reprinted with permission.

CONCLUSION 2. *For spatial models with low candidate dispersion, Condorcet efficiency drops drastically for the Hare, runoff, and single-vote plurality systems, but remains almost unchanged for the other four methods studied.*

From a broader perspective, however, Duverger's law suggests that long-term, single-vote plurality voting may reduce the number of parties and hence the number of candidates. To take account of this effect, we might suppose that the effective Condorcet efficiency of a voting system is an average of Condorcet efficiencies for K candidate elections, weighted by the probability that there will be K candidates. Condorcet efficiency tends to decrease, for all voting systems, as the number of candidates rises. Thus, the effective Condorcet efficiency of single-vote plurality, in general elections, may be higher relative to that of the other systems than is suggested in tables 2.1 and 2.2.

The Condorcet candidate is—for a sufficiently large electorate following a symmetric spatial distribution—that candidate located nearest the center of the distribution of voters. Accordingly, we obtain a third conclusion:

CONCLUSION 3. *Under spatial model assumptions, for multicandidate elections, Condorcet efficiency is a measure of the tendency of centrists to win under a specific electoral system.*

Low Condorcet efficiency of a system suggests that extremists (that is, candidates far from the spatial center) may be more likely to win. This establishes a centrifugal force pushing candidates outward in their efforts to win. Under a procedure enjoying high Condorcet efficiency, candidates espousing centrist views are more likely to win than those expressing more extreme views. In the latter case, there is a centripetal force drawing candidates toward the center.

The relative dispersion of candidates to voters is, then, related to Condorcet efficiency. As candidates move in toward the center, those nearest the center are the victims of a squeeze effect under voting systems for which first preferences are of premium importance—single-vote plurality, and to a lesser extent the Hare and runoff procedures. Centrists are less certain of selection in multicandidate contests under these systems.

One may conjecture that for each electoral system there may be an equilibrium level of relative dispersion of candidates to voters under which all distances from the center would be about equally attractive to additional candidates. According to the simulations reported above, this occurs for the single-vote plurality system when the relative dispersion of candidates to voters is about 0.5 (for five candidates). The simulations further suggest a similar nonconvergent equilibrium for Hare and runoff. For the Black, Coombs, Borda, and approval voting methods, however, the benefits of centrist location are little affected by relative dispersion. For these electoral systems, the center (median) appears likely to be the desired position for winning-oriented candidates under a multicandidate normal spatial model.

The classic median voter result (see McKelvey 1975, Enelow and Hinich 1984) applies only to two-candidate elections using single-vote plurality; in this case equilibrium does occur (under reasonable conditions) at the center (median) position for winning-oriented candidates. Cox (1987), using a unidimensional spatial model shows, however, that in a single-vote plurality election with $K > 2$ candidates, a Nash equilibrium (see Glossary) for candidates, if it exists at all, must include at least one candidate outside the interquartile range of the voter distribution, i.e., at least one of the candidates must be far from the center. If that distribution is further assumed to be uniform on the interval from 0 to 1, Cox proves that no equilibrium exists for K odd. If K is even, he shows that there is a unique Nash equilibrium in which two candidates occur at each of the $K/2$ points $1/K, 3/K, 5/K, \ldots, (K-1)/K$. In other words, in this equilibrium the candidates are almost evenly distributed throughout the spatial interval.

The most striking finding of the Cox paper is that single-vote plurality stands essentially alone among plurality voting systems in not having a median multicandidate equilibrium. Necessary and sufficient conditions are given for the existence of convergent equilibria under classes of voting systems including the Borda count and approval voting. Cox obtains partial results for nonconvergent equilibria. The theorems, presented for unidimensional spatial models, extend to multidimensional models for symmetric voter distributions.

For approval voting, Cox further proves under reasonable assumptions that for a unidimensional spatial model and any $K > 1$, there is a unique Nash equilibrium at the median of the distribution of voters. This result extends to multidimensional spaces if the distribution of voters is symmetric enough to possess a multidimensional median. If no such median exists, then there is no convergent Nash equilibrium. This establishes a striking distinction between candidates' optimal strategies under single-vote plurality and under multivote systems, a distinction that is consonant with the expectations based on simulation.

Following a discussion of social-utility efficiency in chapter 3, we will return in chapter 4 to Condorcet efficiency, investigating the effect of alternative spatial assumptions, such as voter uncertainty about the spatial position of candidates, on the likelihood of selection of the Condorcet candidate. In chapter 6, we will find that the effect of strategic voting necessitates yet another revision of our assessment of the Condorcet efficiency of electoral systems.

3

....

SOCIAL-UTILITY

EFFICIENCY

3.1. INTRODUCTION

A second measure of the tendency of an electoral system to reflect the collective values of the electorate attempts to assess the intensity of support of candidates by the voters. Under the Condorcet criterion, two candidates are compared on the basis of the relative number of voters who prefer each to the other. This criterion, however, ignores the intensity of those preferences. Although strength of preference is in most cases not revealed by votes cast and is difficult to ascertain from actual voters, that is not to say that such intensities do not exist in the minds of the voters. Insofar as a random society or spatial model is a reasonable model of voter opinion, intensities of preference, recovered from simulated data in the form of voter utilities for candidates, are meaningful.

The problem of intensity, in a polity whose hallmark is political equality, has bedeviled political scientists for decades. In simplest terms, the problem is stated by Dahl (1956): should the preferences of a relatively apathetic majority take precedence over the desires of a relatively intense minority. The question is a modern emendation of a longstanding problem of democratic theory: the protection of the rights of minorities.

In a direct clash between only two alternatives, any of the voting systems we have considered will permit the majority to decide, regardless of the intensity of its preferences relative to the intensity of those of the minority. In most actual decision making, however, each alternative (candidate, party, bill) possesses components that voters support at varying levels of intensity. Thus, for example, voters amenable to a pro-choice position on abortion but concerned about many other issues as well may divide their support between two candidates, one of whom holds a pro-choice position and the other an anti-abortion position. By contrast, an anti-abortion minority may, because of its members' intensity of feeling about this single issue, almost unanimously support the antiabortion can-

30

didate while ignoring the consideration of other issues, thereby electing a candidate with whom they agree on their preeminent issue.

In the presence of more than two candidates, some voting procedures permit the voter to transmit intensities of preference to a limited degree. All procedures based on a rank-order ballot, such as the Borda count, the Hare and Coombs methods, and all Condorcet completion methods, permit a voter to convey, however imperfectly, the relative intensities of preferences between candidates through the degree of separation in the preference order. Generally, it would seem that a voter finds more difference between her first and last preferences than between her first and second. Under approval voting, a voter, by adjusting the number of candidates for whom she votes, can indicate a strong preference for a single candidate over all the rest, or, alternatively, a severe dislike for one candidate relative to the others. Accordingly, one might expect that these systems would be more likely to select a candidate whose average utility in the eyes of the voters is high.

As an example, suppose there are three candidates, A, B, and C, and five voters with utilities as shown.

Candidate	3 voters	2 voters
A	100	25
B	75	100
C	0	0

Given that utilities determine preferences, A is preferred to B by three voters to two, and A to C by all five voters; hence, A is the Condorcet candidate.

Candidate B, however, appears to have stronger second-place intensity of support than candidate A. If the ratings are interpreted as Von Neumann–Morgenstern utilities,[1] then the first three voters prefer B to a lottery in which A and C have an equal chance of winning, since the utility of B exceeds the average of the utilities of A and C. Similarly, the last two voters would prefer an equiprobable lottery between B and C over A. Although this type of argument is fraught with difficulty because it involves interpersonal comparisons of utilities, one would expect that B has stronger support than preference orders alone indicate.

One way to attempt to capture this elusive phenomenon is to compare the average utilities of the candidates over all voters. In the example

---

[1] A rating function $u(x)$ is called a Von Neumann–Morgenstern utility if for any probabilities p and q ($p + q = 1$) and two alternatives A and B, $u(pA + qB) = pu(A) + qu(B)$. This relation is expressed in words by saying that the utility of a lottery between A and B with weights p and q is the same as the weighted average of the utilities of A and B, again using the weights p and q.

31

above, these average utilities are 70, 85, and 0, respectively, i.e., B has the highest average utility. Equivalently, we might compare the total utilities for the candidates. Following Harsanyi (1977), I define the *social utility* of a candidate as the sum of all voter utilities for that candidate.[2]

The concept of social-utility efficiency was introduced by Weber (1977) for a random society, although the definition extends (using an appropriate normalization) to spatial models. The idea is to relate the social utility of the candidate selected by an electoral system to that of the candidate whose social utility is highest.

For a fixed voting system, *social-utility efficiency* is defined as the ratio between the expected social utilities of the candidate selected by the system and the candidate that maximizes social utility.[3] Thus social-utility efficiency (*SUE*) is given by the following formula.

$$SUE = \frac{E\,[\text{selected candidate}] \,-\, E\,[\text{random candidate}]}{E\,[\text{maximizing candidate}] \,-\, E\,[\text{random candidate}]}$$

where $E[\ ]$ denotes expected value (long-term average over many replications) of social utility. Note that *SUE* depends on the number n of voters as well as the voting procedure.

For example, if expected social utilities for the random, selected, and maximizing candidates are 50, 65, and 70, respectively, then social-utility efficiency = $(65 - 50)/(70 - 50) = 15/20 = 0.75$. Expected social utilities depend on the number n of voters and the number K of candidates. The ratio will be expressed as a percent by multiplying by 100. Using the laws of probability, Weber (1977) computed exact social-utility efficiencies (in the limit, as the number of voters approaches infinity), for Borda and single-vote plurality for any number of candidates as well as for approval voting for 3 candidates.

3.2. SIMULATION RESULTS FOR SOCIAL-UTILITY EFFICIENCY

Simulated social-utility efficiencies for a random society with $n = 25$ voters are presented in table 3.1 and figure 3.1. As in the case of Condorcet efficiency, simulations were conducted for $K = 3, 4, 5, 7$, and 10 candidates. In each case, 10,000 elections were simulated, with the exception of

---

[2] The concept of social utility need not involve an interpersonal comparison of utilities, as in our example, for it can be equivalently defined in terms of the a priori expected utility of a candidate for a single voter, as suggested by Harsanyi (1977, 48–51).

[3] Each of these expected social utilities is normalized by subtracting the expected social utility of a random candidate in order to discriminate better between the resulting ratios for different systems.

TABLE 3.1. Social-Utility Efficiencies for a Random Society (25 voters)

Voting system	Number of candidates					
	2	3	4	5	7	10
Single-vote plurality	100.0	83.0	75.0	69.2	62.8	53.3
Runoff	100.0	89.5	83.8	80.5	75.6	67.6
Hare	100.0	89.5	84.7	82.4	80.5	74.9
Approval	100.0	95.4	91.1	89.1	87.8	87.0
Borda	100.0	94.8	94.1	94.4	95.4	95.9
Coombs	100.0	89.7	86.7	85.1	83.1	82.4
Black	100.0	93.1	91.9	92.0	93.1	94.3

SOURCE: S. Merrill, "A Comparison of Efficiency of Multicandidate Electoral Systems," *American Journal of Political Science* 28 (1984): 39, Table 3; reprinted with permission.

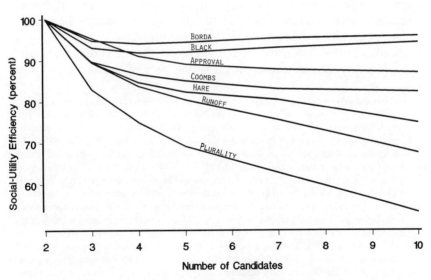

FIGURE 3.1. Social-Utility Efficiency for a Random Society (25 voters).
SOURCE: S. Merrill, "A Comparison of Efficiency of Multicandidate Electoral Systems," *American Journal of Political Science* 28 (1984): 40, Figure 3; reprinted with permission.

the ten-candidate scenario for which 2,500 elections were simulated.[4] The generation of random utilities and optimal strategies under approval voting are described in chapter 2.

Under random-society assumptions, the ranking of the voting systems with respect to social-utility efficiency is almost independent of the number of candidates. In most cases this ranking is Borda, Black, approval, Coombs, Hare, runoff, and single-vote plurality. The Borda, Black, and Coombs methods yield high Condorcet and social-utility efficiencies. For approval voting, however, social-utility efficiency is notably higher than Condorcet efficiency. In general, approval voting performs better with regard to social-utility efficiency, the elimination methods better for Condorcet efficiency.

Social-utility efficiencies under spatial model assumptions are presented in table 3.2 for a five-candidate field and 201 voters. Figures 3.2 and 3.3 give graphs of social-utility efficiency for a two-dimensional spatial model with correlation = 0.5 (201 voters) for relative dispersions of 1.0 and 0.5, respectively.

Provided that candidates and voters have the same variance (relative dispersion = 1.0), social-utility efficiencies for a spatial model are generally higher than for a random society, but the rankings of the voting systems are almost exactly the same. For a more concentrated candidate pattern (relative dispersion = 0.5), social-utility efficiencies for single-vote plurality, Hare, and runoff drop drastically, whereas those for Borda, approval, Coombs, and Black are almost unperturbed.

Bordley (1984) conducted simulations involving social utility for single-vote plurality, Borda, and approval voting, as well as for a Condorcet

---

[4] The standard errors (s.e.) were estimated to be 0.1 to 0.6 percentage points for all voting systems for seven or fewer candidates (and double these values for the 2,500 elections with ten candidates). Simulations with a larger electorate (201 voters) but fewer elections showed changes in efficiency no greater than statistical error. Simulated utilities were normalized by range, i.e., each voter's set of utilities was linearly expanded so that the highest and lowest utilities for each voter were 1 and 0, respectively. This was done so that each voter's opportunity to influence the social utility of candidates would be more nearly equal. A second normalization was performed by replacing personal utilities by their standard scores instead of normalizing by range. The resulting efficiencies differed from those based on range normalizations by only 0.1 to 0.5 percent. Weber (1977) used no normalization of utilities in his calculations. Efficiencies computed by simulation with and without normalization were found to differ only by a constant, which depends on the number of candidates in the field and not on the system of voting. Hence for purposes of comparing voting systems with regard to social-utility efficiency in a random society, the question of normalization is moot. For the spatial model simulations, standard scores were used as the most practical computational method.

TABLE 3.2. Social-Utility Efficiencies under Random Society and Spatial Model
Assumptions (201 voters, 5 candidates)
C = correlation between variates; D = number of dimensions

Voting System	Random society	Spatial model							
		Dispersion = 1.0				Dispersion = 0.5			
		$C = 0.5$		$C = 0.0$		$C = 0.5$		$C = 0.0$	
		$D = 2$	$D = 4$	$D = 2$	$D = 4$	$D = 2$	$D = 4$	$D = 2$	$D = 4$
Single-vote plurality	70	64	75	74	93	−1	0	22	52
Runoff	81	86	92	88	98	28	47	48	75
Hare	82	88	92	91	98	40	59	52	82
Approval	90	96	96	97	98	96	96	95	98
Borda	95	98	98	98	99	97	97	96	99
Coombs	87	96	96	96	98	92	92	92	94
Black	93	97	98	98	99	96	97	96	98

SOURCE: S. Merrill, "A Comparison of Efficiency of Multicandidate Electoral Systems," *American Journal of Political Science* 28 (1984): 41, Table 4; reprinted with permission.

completion method suggested by Copeland.[5] Rather than use a spatial model, he permits nonzero correlation among utilities either across voters or across candidates and assumes optimal strategies for equiprobable outcomes (see section 5.3 below). His results for large electorates indicate the same ranking for plurality voting systems as that in table 3.2 (with the Copeland method attaining efficiencies comparable to those of Black's

[5] The Copeland method specifies that the Condorcet candidate be chosen if one exists. If not, the candidate who wins the most pairwise contests is the winner. This method—although seeming to provide a neat solution to the Condorcet paradox—often yields an indeterminate outcome. If there is no Condorcet winner among three candidates, and no pairwise contest yields a tie (ties are unlikely in mass elections), then each member of the three-cycle wins one pairwise contest. Hence, the Copeland method does not even reduce the size of the indeterminate set of candidates. For four candidates, there are six pairwise contests. Assuming no Condorcet winner and no pairwise ties, each candidate wins no more than two pairwise contests. Since there are six pairwise winners, at least two candidates must each win at least two contests. Hence, at best, for four candidates the Copeland method reduces the size of the indeterminate set from four to two.

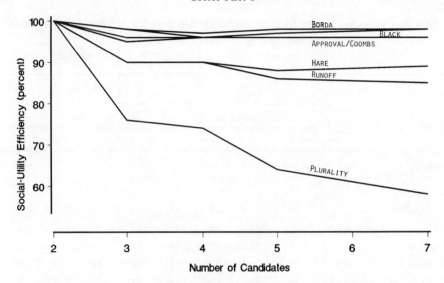

FIGURE 3.2. Social-Utility Efficiency under Spatial Model Assumptions (201 Voters, 2 Dimensions, Correlation = 0.5, Relative Dispersion = 1.0).
SOURCE: S. Merrill, "A Comparison of Efficiency of Multicandidate Electoral Systems," *American Journal of Political Science* 28 (1984): 42, Figure 4.a; reprinted with permission.

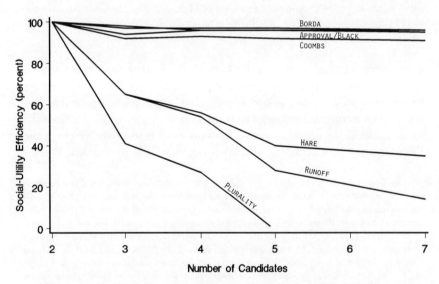

FIGURE 3.3. Social-Utility Efficiency under Spatial Model Assumptions (201 Voters, 2 Dimensions, Correlation = 0.5, Relative Dispersion = 0.5).
SOURCE: S. Merrill, "A Comparison of Efficiency of Multicandidate Electoral Systems," *American Journal of Political Science* 28 (1984): 43, Figure 4.b; reprinted with permission.

method), except that the performance of approval voting drops off markedly with high correlation among voters.

3.3. CONCLUSIONS

The following statements summarize the simulation findings about social-utility efficiency:

CONCLUSION 1. *Social-utility efficiency is highest for the Borda, Black, approval voting, and Coombs procedures; somewhat lower for the Hare and runoff methods; and lowest for single-vote plurality.*

CONCLUSION 2. *The social-utility efficiencies of the Hare, runoff, and single-vote plurality methods drop sharply due to a squeeze effect, as the candidates become more tightly clustered toward the center of the voter distribution.*

The candidate with the maximum social utility (see tables 2.1 and 2.2) is no more likely to be the Condorcet candidate than is the candidate selected by many if not most of the systems studied. That is to say, the Condorcet criterion and the criterion of maximizing social utility are in fact very different.

Looked at from the other side of the coin, however, one sees that the Condorcet candidate generally has high social utility, although she may not have the highest of all candidates. This can be seen by comparing the social-utility efficiencies of the Black and Borda systems. The two systems differ only when there is a Condorcet candidate; the fact that the former has almost as high an efficiency as the latter indicates that the Condorcet candidate has relatively high social utility, although not as high as the Borda winner even when a Condorcet candidate exists.

Not surprisingly, approval voting, the only voting system studied in this chapter that takes account of utilities in addition to preferences to determine optimal strategies (see chapter 5), rates much higher in social-utility efficiency than it does with regard to the Condorcet criterion. On the other hand, the Hare and Coombs procedures, both of which employ a number of comparisons among candidates, have higher Condorcet than social-utility efficiency.

37

4

· · · · · · · · · · · · · · · · · · ·

THE EFFECT OF ALTERNATIVE

SPATIAL MODELS ON CONDORCET

AND SOCIAL-UTILITY EFFICIENCY

4.1. INTRODUCTION

The assumptions for the spatial models in chapters 2 and 3 were necessarily simplistic. In this chapter, I investigate through further simulations a number of variations in these assumptions and their effects on Condorcet and social-utility efficiency. The variations involve alternative spatial distributions of the voters and candidates, the introduction of voters' perceptual uncertainty concerning candidates' positions, alternative utility functions, and a restriction on candidate configuration. The results are taken from Merrill (1985). Because of the limited number of simulations that could be performed, the analysis for some of these variations may be more suggestive than definitive.

Since a single simulation is based on only 1,000 elections, the Condorcet (or social-utility) efficiency estimated directly from that simulation may be less accurate than the estimate for the same parameters obtained from a statistical model calibrated from many simulation runs. Such a model, based on logistic multiple regression, is developed in Appendix A (see formula A.3).

Calibrated from 35,000 simulated elections, this model estimates Condorcet efficiency from three input parameters: (1) the number K of candidates, (2) the relative dispersion, RD, of candidates to voters, and (3) a generalized measure of dimension, GD, which agrees with the ordinary number of dimensions for uncorrelated variates. Because of the greater precision of the model estimates, they will be used in comparing Condorcet efficiency between the basic spatial model and alternative spatial models.

With one exception, the effects on social-utility efficiency of each of the alternative spatial model assumptions studied in this chapter are very similar to the corresponding effects on Condorcet efficiency. For this reason, the results for social-utility efficiency will not be noted separately, except for the consequences of altering the utility function that, predictably, has a differential impact on the two measures of efficiency.

4.2. ALTERNATIVE SPATIAL DISTRIBUTIONS FOR VOTERS AND CANDIDATES

Two variations were investigated for the probability distribution from which voters and candidates were generated. First, the multivariate normal distribution was replaced by a (two-dimensional) uniform distribution on a square. One scenario was run and the resulting changes in Condorcet efficiencies, in comparison with those of the base model, were recorded in table 4.1.[1]

Estimates for Condorcet efficiency for the single-vote plurality and runoff system drop, whereas the estimate for approval voting increases (all

TABLE 4.1. Change in Condorcet Efficiency under Alternative Assumptions Values (for Voting Systems) in Percentage Points; Number of Dimensions = 2

	Uniform distribution	Polarized society		Perceptual uncertainty		City block metric	Shepsle utility	Convex hull
		s.d. = 1.0	s.d. = 0.5	$RD = 1$	$RD = 0.5$			
No. of candidates	5	5	5	5	5	5	5	4
Single-vote plurality	−8	−11	−27	+11	+16	+3	0	−1
Runoff	−7	−11	−24	+14	+36	0	0	+1
Hare	−2	−10	−26	+16	+44	+2	0	+2
Approval	+9	+1	+1	+9	+6	0	+11	+11
Borda	+1	−2	−18	+5	+5	−3	0	+1
Coombs	−2	0	−10	+1	+3	−2	0	−1

SOURCE: S. Merrill, "A Statistical Model for Condorcet Efficiency based on Simulation under Spatial Model Assumptions," *Public Choice* 47 (1985): 395, Table 3; adapted with permission.

[1] This scenario involved five candidates, $RD = 1$, and one thousand elections. The results were compared with the model estimates from the logistic multiple regression formula (A.3) for a two-dimensional multivariate normal distribution with uncorrelated variates.

significant at the 0.05 level). As noted in section 2.3, for any symmetric distribution, the Condorcet winner is ordinarily the candidate nearest the center of the distribution. Such a candidate tends to be squeezed by neighboring candidates under the single-vote plurality and runoff systems. This tendency should be relatively more severe under the uniform distribution, which unlike the normal distribution has no compensating "hump" of voters at the center. The simulation results bear out this expectation.

Distributions of voters in polarized societies or dual cultures have two or more humps (see the Glossary for definitions and Rabushka and Shepsle 1972, and Dutter 1982, for further discussion). My simulations for a polarized society use an (equal) mixture of two (two-dimensional) normal distributions (each with uncorrelated variates) centered at the points $(-1, 0)$ and $(+1, 0)$, respectively.[2]

The results (see table 4.1) suggest that Condorcet efficiency drops sharply with increasing polarization of the electorate, especially for the Borda, single-vote plurality, runoff, and Hare systems. It is not hard to see that (for RD near unity) the last three systems mentioned tend to choose a candidate near one of the poles and hence are less likely to choose a Condorcet candidate near the center of the mixed distribution. Centrist candidates tend to receive many middle ranks under the Borda count and are less likely to win than under a unimodal distribution. Under approval voting in a polarized society, centrist candidates tend to do at least as well as polar candidates, although the margin of victory may be small and hence unstable. In a polarized electorate, furthermore, many approval voters might plausibly deviate from their optimal strategies by refusing to vote for a centrist candidate, so that the simulation probably overestimates the Condorcet efficiency of approval voting.

Broadly speaking, the results can be described as follows:

CONCLUSION 1. *A uniform distribution of voters accentuates the squeeze effect by offering no centrist hump of voters, reducing the Condorcet efficiency of the single-vote plurality, Hare, and runoff systems.*

CONCLUSION 2. *Condorcet efficiency may drop sharply in a polarized society as the poles attract voters away from centrist candidates.*

4.3. PERCEPTUAL UNCERTAINTY OF CANDIDATES' POSITIONS

I turn now to the effect of voters' perceptual uncertainty of the candidates' spatial positions. Empirical data support the common-sense notion that

[2] Two scenarios were run (each with five candidates and $RD = 1.0$): one with standard deviation (s.d.) = 1.0 (in which the mixed multivariate density forms a ridge between the poles), and one with s.d. = 0.5 (here the mixed density exhibits distinct peaks at the poles).

voters, even those capable of locating the candidates spatially, do not agree on the positions of candidates. Aldrich and McKelvey's empirical analysis (1977, tables 4 and 5, 121–22) suggests that the variation in voters' perceptions of candidates' positions (in standard deviations) for certain issues (the war in Vietnam and urban unrest) in the 1968 and 1972 presidential elections ranged from about 0.2 to 0.6 (where the standard deviations of voter positions are normalized to unity).

For purposes of simulation, I assume that for each voter, each candidate position is perturbed by a multivariate normal distribution with the same parameters as those from which voters and candidates were generated, but with the standard deviation along each dimension (issue) multiplied by a parameter s, representing perceptual uncertainty. Effectively, this replaces each candidate's ideal point with a smear whose dimensions are reflected in the quantity s.

A two-dimensional model with correlation $= 0.5$ was assumed. Using $s = 0.5$ (reflecting fairly high perceptual uncertainty in light of the Aldrich–McKelvey data) and $K = 5$, Condorcet efficiency increases sharply (relative to that for no uncertainty) for the single-vote plurality, runoff, and Hare systems, and slightly for approval voting and the Borda count.

Perceptual uncertainty, as measured by the parameter s, effectively increases the relative dispersion, increasing it to equal the square root of $(RD^2 + s^2)$. However, this factor is insufficient to account for the increases in Condorcet efficiency under perceptual uncertainty, particularly for the Hare and runoff systems. It appears that under these systems, a centrist (Condorcet) candidate may avert early elimination by the surrounding candidates and have a good chance of winning after the field is winnowed, if each candidate's position is effectively smeared over a wider territory through perceptual uncertainty. Apparently, it is much more difficult for such a candidate to win under single-vote plurality on the first ballot. A squeeze is not disadvantageous for the approval voting, Borda, and Coombs systems, so perceptual uncertainty has less effect in these systems.

Additional simulation runs suggest that the increase in Condorcet efficiency is much less as we reduce the parameter s for perceptual uncertainty from 0.5 to 0.25. On the other hand, no further increase in Condorcet efficiency occurs if we raise the parameter above 0.5.

The simulation results are summarized in the following statement:

CONCLUSION 3. *Perceptual uncertainty of candidates' positions, by blurring the squeeze effect, produces a marked increase in Condorcet efficiency for the single-vote plurality, Hare, and runoff systems.*

41

CHAPTER 4

4.4. ALTERNATIVE UTILITY FUNCTIONS

It might be argued that (Euclidean) distance between voter and candidate is less appropriate in defining utility than a metric that adds absolute deviations over dimensions: the *city-block metric*, given by $\Sigma|v_i - c_i|$, where $v = (v_1, \ldots, v_m)$ and $c = (c_1, \ldots, c_m)$ are the voter's and the candidate's positions, respectively and m = number of dimensions. Under the city-block metric, a voter has the same utility for a candidate with whom he differs by one unit (standard deviation) on each of two issues as for a candidate who agrees with him on one issue, but differs from him on the other issue by two units. By contrast, for the Euclidean metric, the voter would be indifferent between these candidates if the second differed by only the square root of two units on one issue.

The city-block metric is not rotation invariant. One simulation run using the city-block metric (see table 4.1) suggests that Condorcet efficiency is not significantly affected by replacing the Euclidean with the city-block metric.

Since Condorcet efficiency appears insensitive to the exact definition of the metric, I now return to the Euclidean metric for convenience. I consider an alternative utility function in which we replace the negative of distance with the normal density function applied to the distance, as suggested by Shepsle (1972). This function, which I will refer to as the *Shepsle utility function*, is given by

$$u(d) = \exp(-d^2/2),$$

in contrast to the *negative-of-distance utility function*,

$$u(d) = -d,$$

where d is the Euclidean distance from voter to candidate. A theoretical justification for the use of the Shepsle utility function is given in Appendix B.

The Shepsle utility was used in a simulation run with dimension 2 and correlation = 0.5. Except for approval voting, voting depends only on preference order and hence is unaffected by alteration of the utility function, as long as the preference order is unperturbed. For $RD = 1.0$, Condorcet efficiency for approval voting increases significantly (see table 4.1). The resulting Condorcet efficiency for single-vote plurality is 57 percent, while those for other systems range from 78 to 100 percent. For $RD = 0.5$, no significant changes occur.

This pattern is to be expected. Whenever there is one extreme candidate, all other candidates rate above average under the negative-of-distance utility for most voters. Hence, the winner is distinguished by a small

42

margin of voters, leading to unstable results. The Shepsle utility amelio-rates this problem, leading to what I believe are more realistic results. The Shepsle utility function also appears to reflect a more plausible distribu-tion of voter utilities than the negative-of-distance function (see Appendix B). Results for Condorcet efficiency are summarized in the following state-ment:

CONCLUSION 4. *Incorporation of the Shepsle utility function into the base model, which dampens the drop-off in utility for low-ranked candi-dates, increases the Condorcet efficiency of approval voting.*

The Shepsle utility function has a different effect on social-utility effi-ciency, which increases by 6 to 13 percentage points for the single-vote plurality, Hare, and runoff systems, but is unchanged for the other pro-cedures. Under the simulation conditions described above, the Shepsle utility produces a social-utility efficiency of 77 percent for single-vote plu-rality, whereas the corresponding efficiencies for all the other systems fall in a tight cluster between 93 and 98 percent.

CONCLUSION 5. *Although the social-utility efficiency of single-vote plurality increases under the Shepsle utility function, it is still distinctly lower than that of all of the other systems.*

4.5. A RESTRICTION ON CANDIDATE CONFIGURATION

Random generation of candidates results in a large number of candidate sets in which all candidates are to one side of the voter median. Such a sit-uation appears politically unstable and perhaps unrealistic. Accordingly, two simulations were run[3] in which all simulated candidate sets whose convex hull[4] failed to contain the center were discarded. No significant changes in Condorcet efficiency occur except for approval voting, for which Condorcet efficiency increases about ten percentage points (signif-icant at the 0.05 level) in each scenario. Approval voting tends to select a candidate between the center of the sample of candidates generated and the center of the voters.[5] If the candidates are strongly skewed to one side, approval voting is unlikely to choose the Condorcet candidate.

[3] Both runs assume two dimensions and correlation $= 0.5$. One uses $K = 4$ and $RD = 1$; the other, $K = 7$ and $RD = 0.5$.
[4] The *convex hull* of a set of points (candidates) in K-dimensional space is the smallest con-vex body containing these points. It consists of all line segments connecting pairs of the points, all line segments connecting points so generated, and so forth.
[5] Suppose, for example, in a one-dimensional model using the negative-of-distance utility function, that all candidates are to the right of the voter median, in positions $0 < c_1 < c_2 <$

CONCLUSION 6. *If lopsided candidate configurations are discarded, the Condorcet efficiency of approval voting increases.*

4.6. COMPARISON OF MODELS

The existence of perceptual uncertainty in real elections and the argument for a utility function something like a normal density are, I believe, the most compelling reasons for alteration of the basic model. Table 4.2 presents a comparison of Condorcet efficiency for 5 candidates and 2 dimensions (correlation = 0.5) between the basic logistic regression model (A.3) and simulation runs that also incorporate perceptual uncertainty (parameter = 0.5) and the Shepsle utility.

TABLE 4.2. Comparison of Condorcet Efficiency for Base Model and Scenarios Modified by Perceptual Uncertainty and the Shepsle Utility

System	RD = 1.0		RD = 0.5	
	Base model	Modified model	Base model	Modified model
Single-vote plurality	57	60	24	45
Runoff	78	88	34	73
Hare	78	90	36	79
Approval	72	85	70	76
Borda	86	89	83	88
Coombs	95	95	89	93

SOURCE: S. Merrill, "A Statistical Model for Condorcet Efficiency Based on Simulation under Spatial Model Assumptions," *Public Choice* 47 (1985): 400, Table 6; reprinted with permission.

$\ldots < c_K$. Let c_L be the candidate just to the left of the candidate mean. Since a voter's optimal strategy is to vote for any candidate whose distance is less than the mean distance to all candidates, all voters to the left of c_1 (a majority of all voters) vote for each of $c_1, \ldots, c_L$. As we move in the voter spectrum to the right of c_1, voters cease to vote for c_1 at some point p_1, cease to vote for c_2 at p_2, etc. Clearly $p_1 \leq p_2 \leq \ldots \leq p_L$. Candidates c_i for $i > L$ receive no votes from voters to the left of the voter median and cannot attain a majority of ballots. Thus, except for the possibility of ties, the largest approval vote is obtained by candidate c_L, who is often nearer the candidate mean than the voter median. If we assume, instead, the Shepsle utility, the winning candidate tends to be somewhat closer to the voter median.

For relative dispersion = 1.0, the most striking feature of the modified model is the low Condorcet efficiency for the single-vote plurality system in contrast to the uniformly high values for the other five systems. Even for low relative dispersion ($RD = 0.5$), Condorcet efficiencies under the modified model for these same five systems—which range from 73 to 93 percent—are all markedly higher than that for single-vote plurality (45 percent). Condorcet efficiencies for the Hare and runoff systems, however, are very sensitive to the level of perceptual uncertainty, dropping sharply as uncertainty declines.

4.7. CONCLUSIONS

We have investigated several alternative spatial model assumptions by comparing simulation estimates for Condorcet and social-utility efficiency with those predicted by a logistic regression model for comparable multivariate normal assumptions. We find that use of a city-block (as opposed to a Euclidean) metric has no significant effect on Condorcet efficiency. Using the Shepsle utility function (as opposed to the negative-of-distance utility function) affects only approval voting, increasing Condorcet efficiency by about ten percentage points. Ruling inadmissible those candidate configurations whose convex hull omits the center of the distribution of voters has much the same effect, again only on approval voting.

When perceptual uncertainty of candidates' positions is incorporated into the model, a resulting sharp increase is found in Condorcet efficiency for the single-vote plurality, runoff, and Hare systems, and a modest increase for approval voting and the Borda count, due apparently to amelioration of the squeeze effect. Replacement of a multivariate normal distribution by a uniform distribution produces an increase in Condorcet efficiency for approval voting, but reductions for the single-vote plurality and runoff systems. Polarizing the electorate by the use of a bimodal distribution leads to sharp decreases for the single-vote plurality, Hare, runoff, and Borda count systems. These alternative assumptions, except for the Shepsle utility function, have similar effects on social-utility efficiency.

In summary, with respect to the various alternatives considered in this chapter, the approval voting and Coombs systems appear to be the most robust to reduction in Condorcet and social-utility efficiency due to variations in spatial model assumptions. In the presence of perceptual uncertainty, the Coombs and Borda systems have the highest Condorcet efficiency, although all systems other than single-vote plurality have relatively high values for both Condorcet and social-utility efficiency.

45

CHAPTER 4

The consistently low Condorcet efficiency of single-vote plurality voting—the electoral system most commonly used in English speaking countries—raises serious questions for its continued use in multicandidate elections. Our evaluation must, however, await a major reassessment in chapter 6, where strategic voting is taken into account.

5

. . . .

STRATEGIC VOTING UNDER

PLURALITY ELECTORAL SYSTEMS:

DECISIONS UNDER UNCERTAINTY

AND UNDER RISK

5.1. INTRODUCTION

In any electoral system, many voters intuitively try to take into account expected candidate strengths as well as their own preferences in determining how to vote. This phenomenon is perhaps best known in the case of single-vote plurality, where it may be optimal for a voter to vote for a second or third choice if that candidate is perceived as having a better chance of winning. This strategy—if exercised by many voters—leads to the desertion of trailing candidates and no doubt explains much of the drop in popular vote support for George Wallace in the 1972 U.S. presidential election (from a high of 21 percent in the September polls to 14 percent in the actual vote on election day in November) and for John Anderson in the 1980 presidential election (from a high of 23 percent in an April poll to 7 percent on election day).

Under the approval voting system, a voter who prefers a trailing candidate may vote both for her favorite and for her preference among the front-runners. Although the voter need not forsake her true preference, she must decide on the number of candidates for whom to vote. Rationally this strategic decision entails optimizing the voter's influence on the outcome.

Naively, one might think that that influence would be increased simply by voting for more candidates. But the voter exercises influence by making distinctions between candidates; the most distinctions are made by voting for about half the candidates. In an election, for example, with four candidates A, B, C, and D, voting just for A makes three distinctions: between

47

A and B, A and C, and A and D. Voting for A, B, and C (i.e., not voting for D) also involves three distinctions. By contrast, a ballot for exactly two, say A and B, makes four distinctions: between A and C, A and D, B and C, and B and D. A voter who votes for all the candidates makes no distinctions whatever, and has no influence on the relative standings of the candidates.

This vote-for-half strategy may need to be modified, however, because some distinctions may be more valuable to the voter than others. For example, distinctions between candidates who differ greatly in utility and—with knowledge of others' expected votes—distinctions between front-runners would appear to be more profitable than others. Thus the optimal strategy may involve the expansion or contraction of the vote-for-half criterion, or it may even involve skipping a candidate to vote for one of lower utility. I will present evidence that of these strategies, contraction of the voting set is most likely to benefit the voter, while skipping a candidate appears to be the least likely to benefit the voter.

The Borda count opens a Pandora's box of problems for strategic manipulation. The voter can use the system to separate, say, two front-runners as much as possible by giving the highest score to the preferred front-runner and the lowest score to the other. In some cases, winning may depend on inducing one's supporters to manipulate in this manner. If manipulation of this type is sufficiently widespread, a trailing candidate may, perversely, sneak through to victory by tallying sufficient "in-between" scores.

The following example of the potential of strategic voting under the Borda count is patterned on the U.S. presidential election. Suppose there are 100 votes (each representing one percent of the national electorate) and three candidates: a Democrat, a Republican, and a minor party candidate.

Rank	Borda score	52 voters	48 voters
1	2	Democrat	Republican
2	1	Republican	Democrat
3	0	Minor party	Minor party

Under sincere Borda voting, the Democrat would win with a total Borda score of 152 to 148 for the Republican and 0 for the minor party. Suppose, however, that one-fourth of the Democrats (13 voters) and one-half of the Republicans (24 voters) were willing to vote insincerely; that is, to vote as if they ranked the candidates as follows:

Rank	Borda score	13 voters	39 voters	24 voters	24 voters
1	2	Democrat	Democrat	Republican	Republican
2	1	Minor party	Republican	Minor party	Democrat
3	0	Republican	Minor party	Democrat	Minor party

Now the Republican wins with a total Borda score (number of votes) of 135 to 128 for the Democrat and 37 for the minor party. Thus differential insincere voting can reverse the outcome of the election in favor of the party with the greater number of adherents willing to vote insincerely. In fact the algebraic change in the margin between the two major parties (11 votes in this example) is exactly equal to the difference in the number of their insincere adherents. The focus of the contest might shift from one of gathering support for one's candidacy to one of persuading supporters to vote insincerely. If we take the example a step further by assuming that all major party voters vote strategically and include, say, four partisans for the minor party (taken equally from each of the two major parties), then we get political nonsense.

Rank	Borda score	46 voters	2 voters	50 voters	2 voters
1	2	Democrat	Minor party	Republican	Minor party
2	1	Minor party	Democrat	Minor party	Republican
3	0	Republican	Republican	Democrat	Democrat

The minor party, with only 4 supporters, wins the election with 104 votes to 102 for the Republican and 94 for the Democrat! This vulnerability to manipulation calls into question any use of Borda voting in public elections.

We will determine the optimal strategies for a variety of voting systems that use the plurality decision rule, including the three introduced in chapter 1—single-vote plurality, approval voting, and the Borda count. Voters will be assumed capable of assigning utilities (i.e., ratings on an interval or numerical scale) to candidates. Voter decision criteria may involve risk (in which the voter attaches probabilities to the possible outcomes) or uncertainty (in which the voter is assumed to have no knowledge of these probabilities). Under risk, the *relative* strengths of the candidates must be assessed by the voter.

The effect of strategic voting, assuming ordinal preferences, will be studied in chapter 6 for each of the seven voting systems introduced in chapter 1. In chapter 6, optimal strategies will be used to estimate the effect various voting systems might have had on historical elections, assuming voters had used these strategies for each system. Strategic behavior for approval voting under alternative decision rules will be considered in chapter 7. Chapter 9 will deal with the characterization of voting systems that are minimal in the sense that all permissible strategies are potentially optimal under appropriate circumstances.

5.2. A MODEL FOR COMPUTING OPTIMAL STRATEGIES

Consider a plurality voting system in which there are n voters and K candidates $c_i, i = 1, \ldots, K$, one of whom is to be chosen. Denote by $v_i, i = 1, \ldots, K$, the number of votes cast by a focal voter for candidates $c_i, i = 1, \ldots, K$. In general the v_i may be any real numbers. A vector $V = (v_1, \ldots, v_K)$ of votes permissible under a particular system (in a K-candidate election) will be called a *permissible strategy*. Thus a voting system can be identified with the subset S of points in K-dimensional space consisting of permissible strategies for that system. Particular voting systems will usually be specified by placing constraints on the permissible values of v_i (all voters will be subject to the same constraints).

For example, under single-vote plurality, one of the v_i may be 1, but the others must be 0. The Borda count permits each voter to assign the integers $K-1, K-2, \ldots, 0$ in a one-to-one fashion to the K candidates. Under approval voting, each v_i must be either 0 or 1. Those candidates for which $v_i = 1$ constitute the set of candidates for whom the focal voter votes.

I consider here two further plurality voting systems, which, as we will see in chapter 9, have a special relationship to single-vote plurality voting and approval voting, respectively. The first, *cumulative voting* (see Blair 1973), requires that a positive number M be chosen, applicable to each voter, such that $\Sigma v_i \leqslant M$ and $v_i \geqslant 0, i = 1, \ldots, K$. This is analogous to the procedure commonly used in electing members of a corporation board of directors, in which each voter is allowed to apportion a number of votes as she pleases among the candidates. I assume, however, a single winner and an equal number of votes for each voter. The second system, *cardinal-measure voting*, is also called *interval voting* (see Joslyn 1976) or *Bentham's method* (see Riker 1982a). Two positive integers $M_1 < M_2$ are chosen, applicable to each voter, and it is required that $M_1 \leqslant v_i \leqslant M_2, i = 1, \ldots, K$. For example, the voter might be asked to rate candidates on a scale from $M_1 = 0$ to $M_2 = 100$.

I shall address the following question: Given a particular voting system, how might the voter choose the v_i in order to maximize her influence or power on the outcome of the election? A strategy that maximizes a voter's influence in an appropriate sense will be referred to as an *optimal strategy*.

My approach will fall under the heading of decision analysis; in particular I will investigate the optimal decision or strategy for the voter under *uncertainty* and under *risk*, i.e., under different assumptions concerning the voter's knowledge of the likely outcome of the election.

If we assume that the voter has no knowledge of the likelihood of success of the various candidates, the voter is said to be making a decision under uncertainty. The *Savage regret* (minimax regret) or *Laplace* (Bayes) methods may therefore be appropriate (see Luce and Raiffa 1957, pp. 280, 298). If, on the other hand, the voter is capable of assigning subjective probabilities to the relative likelihood of success of the candidates, she is said to face a decision under risk. A decision based on *maximizing expected utility* may then be appropriate.

A voter's knowledge typically lies in-between these two extremes representing no information and complete information. Accordingly, I investigate each type of decision criterion. Furthermore, the assignment of subjective probabilities in order to make decisions under risk permits a continuous gradation between knowledge and uncertainty. As the voter's information approaches complete ignorance, her probabilities approach an equiprobable assignment in which all outcomes occur with equal likelihood. A decision under this latter assignment is, by definition, by the method of Laplace in the face of uncertainty.

The following observation will provide us some opportunity to discriminate between decisions under uncertainty and under risk. For the model and voting systems considered here, the optimal strategies under uncertainty are in most cases sincere reflections of the voter's rankings of the candidates. For decisions under risk, however, this need not be the case. Ferejohn and Fiorina have indicated that this difference in the nature of optimal strategies "affords the possibility of a critical test between minimax regret and maximizing expected utility criteria" (Ferejohn and Fiorina 1974, p. 534).

Under single-vote plurality, the typical insincere optimal strategy involves deserting one's first choice. Under uncertainty, however, the optimal strategy—voting for one's favorite—is always sincere. By exploiting this difference in optimal strategies for the two types of decision criteria, J. Black (1978) and Cain (1978) have each presented guarded empirical support for the criterion of decision under risk and hence of the expected utility model. In particular, Cain (1978) found a significant positive relation between a third-party vote and the differential between the major party vote totals in a sample of British constituencies in 1970. This result suggests that third-party supporters tend to desert their candidate and vote for one of the two main parties when the major party race is close.

51

For the remainder of the chapter, we make the following standing assumptions: the focal voter can associate utilities u_i to the candidates c_i and exercises power only if her vote(s) are decisive, i.e., for some pair of candidates she brings about a win for one of the pair that would not have occurred had she abstained (ties are assumed resolved by lot). The focal voter has an opportunity to be decisive only if some pair of candidates stand sufficiently close in the total votes cast by the other voters. Such a circumstance, in which the focal voter can be decisive, will be referred to as a *contingency*. If the voter is decisive by engendering a win for c_i over c_j, which would not have occurred had she abstained, she receives a payoff of $(u_i - u_j)$.

5.3. DECISIONS UNDER UNCERTAINTY

The Savage regret method chooses that strategy $V = (v_1, \ldots, v_K)$ which minimizes the maximum regret (over all contingencies) that might be suffered for a given decision. Regret is computed relative to the best payoff that could be achieved for a particular contingency.

For example, under approval voting, if there are three candidates A, B, and C, rated in that order, it is easy to check that only voting strategies $\{A\}$ and $\{A, B\}$ are *admissible*, i.e., are undominated by any other strategy. (A voting strategy is said to *dominate* another if the payoff for the former is as good as or better than that for the latter for every contingency and strictly better for some contingency.) Since decisions do not depend on changes of scale or position of the set of utilities (or ratings), we may assume, without loss of generality, that the utilities satisfy

$$1 = u_1 \geqslant u_2 \geqslant u_3 = 0.$$

For simplicity, denote the contingency of a tie (had the focal voter abstained) between, say, candidates A and C by AC. The payoff and regret matrices are given in table 5.1. For example, under contingency AB, if the voter votes only for A, she secures a win for A instead of a tie between A and B, thus attaining a utility gain of $(1 - u_2)/2$. For simplicity, all entries in the matrix have been multiplied by 2. This has no effect on strategy.

It follows that the maximal regret is minimized by strategy $\{A\}$ if $u_2 < 0.5$ and by strategy $\{A, B\}$ if $u_2 > 0.5$. Thus, under this criterion the voter should vote only for candidate A if $u_2 < 0.5$ and for A and B if $u_2 > 0.5$ (the voter would be indifferent between these two options if $u_2 = 0.5$). That this result remains true for the general K-candidate race follows from the following theorem, in which the candidates are ordered so that $u_1 \geqslant u_2 \geqslant \ldots \geqslant u_K$. The theorem also provides optimal strategies for the single-vote plurality and Borda count methods.

TABLE 5.1. Payoff and Regret Matrices for
Three-Candidate Approval Voting

	Contingency				Contingency			Maximal
	AB	AC	BC		AB	AC	BC	regret
Strategy: {A}	$1 - u_2$	1	0	{A}	0	0	u_2	u_2
{A, B}	0	1	u_2	{A, B}	$1 - u_2$	0	0	$1 - u_2$
	PAYOFF MATRIX				MATRIX OF REGRETS			

SOURCE: S. Merrill, "Strategic Voting in Multicandidate Elections under Uncertainty and under Risk," in *Power, Voting, and Voting Power*, ed. M. Holler, 180, unnumbered figure. Copyright 1981 by Physica-Verlag; reprinted with permission.

THEOREM 5.1. In a K-candidate race, the optimal strategies under the criterion of Savage regret are:

(a) Single-vote plurality: Vote for one's first choice.
(b) Borda: Assign votes in order of preference.
(c) Approval: Vote for all candidates c_i for whom $u_i > (u_1 + u_K)/2$.

PROOF. See Appendix C.

Thus, under approval voting, the optimal strategy is to vote for those candidates one rates better than the average of the most preferred and least preferred. For each of the three plurality systems, the optimal strategy under the Savage regret criterion reflects the true rankings of the voter and is hence sincere.

An alternative method for making decisions under uncertainty, known as the Laplace method, treats all contingencies as equally likely, i.e., equiprobable, and determines the expected utility of the payoffs (i.e., the average payoff over all contingencies) for each possible strategy. The criterion then chooses that strategy for which this expected utility is largest.

For example, for approval voting and three candidates, the expected utility for strategy {A} is $(2 - u_2)/3$ and for strategy {A, B} is $(1 + u_2)/3$. Thus strategy {A} is chosen over {A, B} when $(2 - u_2)/3 > (1 + u_2)/3$, i.e., when $u_2 < 0.5$, just as under the Savage regret method. However, for $K > 3$, the Laplace criterion is slightly different from the Savage criterion: An approval voter should vote for all candidates whose utility exceeds the average for all candidates (see Weber 1977, Merrill 1979, or Theorem 5.3 below) rather than the average of the utilities of the most and the least preferred. For the single-vote plurality and Borda count systems, the optimal strategies under the Savage regret and Laplace criteria are the same.

In summary, we have seen that both decision criteria under uncertainty, Savage regret and Laplace, specify that the voter use a sincere strategy. In fact, for the single-vote plurality, Borda count, and approval voting systems, optimal strategies under the two criteria are identical, except in the case of approval voting for more than three candidates. Even here, the strategies differ only slightly, each using a mean of utilities as the cutpoint to separate the approved and disapproved sets of candidates.

5.4. Decisions under Risk

In section 5.3 we considered the voter's optimal strategy for a variety of plurality voting systems as a decision under uncertainty, i.e., under the assumption that the voter has no knowledge of the relative strengths of the candidates and hence of the likely outcome of a political contest. We saw, however, evidence that, for many voters, this assumption is not true. In the present section, I assume that voters are sufficiently sophisticated so as to have some knowledge of and to take account of candidate strengths in determining how to vote.

In mass elections, such knowledge may come from published polls, articles in the press and media, special interest groups, and the candidates' campaigns themselves. Of course, this information may be misleading, some of it deliberately so. In a more restricted electorate, such as a legislature, council, or convention, voters may be expected to know the likely votes of others through direct contact, previous voting patterns, or through the efforts of leaders or whips. At best, in any case, the voter's knowledge of candidate strengths must be expressed in terms of probabilities.

Accordingly, I assume that the focal voter is capable of forming subjective estimates of the strengths of the candidates among other voters, or more precisely, of the relative likelihood of being decisive for each pair of candidates.[1] For a given voting system, let t_{ij} denote the focal voter's subjective estimate of the conditional probability, given that there is a tie, that she be decisive for candidates c_i and c_j by casting exactly one vote for c_i (or for c_j) instead of abstaining. Set $t_{ii} = 0$. Thus the t_{ij} are normalized so that

$$\sum_{i<j}\sum t_{ij} = 1,$$

---

[1] In each system, the total number of votes received by each candidate will be modeled as a random variable, i.e., a variable whose values depend on certain probabilities.

that is, given that there is a tie for first place, t_{ij} is the conditional probability that the tie is between candidates c_i and c_j. I assume that the probabilities of a three-way tie and of more than one tie are neglibile relative to the probability of a single two-way tie; these are reasonable assumptions for any large electorate.

In a tightly contested three-candidate election, a voter might set $t_{11} = t_{12} = t_{23} = 1/3$ (and $t_{ji} = t_{ij}$), i.e., consider each of the three possible two-way ties equally likely. On the other hand, in a three-candidate race in which, say, candidate c_2 appeared to have a slight lead over c_3 and a moderate lead over c_1, probabilities $t_{23} = 1/2$, $t_{12} = 1/3$, and $t_{13} = 1/6$ might be appropriate, as indicated in the following table where t_{ij} is the entry in the ith row and the jth column.

	c_1	c_2	c_3
c_1:	0	1/3	1/6
c_2:	1/3	0	1/2
c_3:	1/6	1/2	0

This example will be referred to repeatedly to illustrate expected utility calculations.

I realize that many voters possess neither the ability nor the inclination to make such estimates. With this in mind, I will consider simplifications of these estimates. In addition, it is ultimately only the optimal strategies, not the probabilities themselves, that need be approximated. With the analytic form of these strategies in hand, I will discuss the difficulties in approximating intuitively the optimal strategies implied by these probabilities. In any event, I believe that knowledge of a voter's optimal strategy under a number of different scenarios (i.e., choices of sets of values t_{ij}) will shed light on her potential behavior.

If the focal voter casts v_i votes for c_i and v_j votes for c_j instead of abstaining, her probability of being decisive is approximately

$$t_{ij}(v_i - v_j)$$

since in the presence of a large number of voters, her probability of reversing the result is approximately proportional to the difference in the number of votes cast for c_i and c_j. If we assume that u_i denotes the utility of the focal voter for candidate c_i, $i = 1, \ldots, K$, then $(u_i - u_j)$ denotes her payoff if she is decisive between c_i and c_j. By summing over all pairs i and j, we obtain the expected utility for vote $V = (v_1, \ldots, v_K)$ in the following display:

$$U(V) = \sum_{i<j} \sum t_{ij}(v_i - v_j)(u_i - u_j). \tag{5.1}$$

55

By rearranging summations, we may represent $U(V)$ as a linear function of $v_1, \ldots, v_K$:

THEOREM 5.2. The expected utility for vote $V = (v_1, \ldots, v_K)$ is given by:

$$U(V) = \sum_{i=1}^{K} S(c_i)v_i, \qquad (5.2)$$

where

$$S(c_i) = \sum_{j=1}^{K} t_{ij}(u_i - u_j). \qquad (5.3)$$

The quantity $S(c_i)$ is, for each i, called the *strategic value* of candidate c_i and represents the expected utility accruing to one incremental vote for candidate c_i.

PROOF. See Appendix C.

Suppose in the example introduced above that the focal voter has utilities as given in the following table.

	u_i	$S(c_i)$
c_1:	1.00	0.250
c_2:	0.75	0.292
c_3:	0.00	-0.542

The quantities $S(c_i)$, computed by formula (5.3), indicate that for the focal voter an incremental vote for c_2 (who is more likely to be in a tie for first place) is more efficacious than one for c_1, despite the higher utility for the latter candidate.

We can now state the optimal strategies under risk for plurality electoral systems. For a voter under the single-vote plurality system, it is clear that by Theorem 5.2, $U(V)$ is maximized if the voter casts her one vote for that candidate for whom $S(c_i)$ is largest, for it is only that term that will appear in the summation in (5.2).[2] In the example above, the candidate for

---

[2] This condition is also equivalent to voting for that candidate for whom

$$t_i[u_i - \sum_{j=1}^{K} (t_{ij}/2t_i)\,u_j]$$

is a maximum, where

whom $S(c_i)$ is largest is c_2. If all candidates are judged equally likely to tie for first place, so that all t_{ij} are equal, this criterion is equivalent to that of Laplace discussed in section 5.3 under the rubric of uncertainty. In this special case, the criterion selects the voter's first choice and is hence a sincere strategy.

Under approval voting, Theorem 5.2 implies that the optimal strategy is to vote for precisely those candidates c_i for whom $S(c_i) > 0$. This follows since $v_i = 1$, if and only if the voter votes for candidate c_i. Thus $U(V) = \Sigma\, S(c_i)$, where the sum is over only those c_i for whom the voter votes. This sum is maximized if only candidates are included for which $S(c_i) > 0$. Candidates for whom $S(c_i)$ equals 0 may be voted for without affecting the value of expected utility.

In the example, strategies $\{c_2\}$ and $\{c_1\}$ yield expected utilities 0.292 and 0.250, respectively. But the optimal strategy $\{c_1, c_2\}$, consisting of voting for all candidates with positive strategic value, offers a higher expected utility of $0.250 + 0.292 = 0.542$. The approval voter attains her highest utility, for this example, by voting not only for her first choice (c_1) but also for her second choice (c_2), who is more likely to be in the race for first place. In general, the rational approval voter should vote for candidates whose utilities exceed a certain weighted average of all the voter's utilities.[3] This result for approval voting was obtained independently by Merrill (1979) and Hoffman (1982).

Note that under some circumstances a rational approval voter might vote for only one or all but one candidate in a large field (e.g., if $K = 5$, all t_{ij} are equal, and $(u_1, \ldots, u_5) = (10,3,2,1,0)$ or $(10,9,8,7,0)$ respectively). For a more typical distribution of utilities, the optimal strategy would involve voting for about half the candidates (see also Fishburn and Brams 1981a).

According to my definition, the optimal strategy maximizes the likelihood that the voter makes a pivot valuable to her interests. This likelihood

---

$$t_i = \sum_{m=1}^{K} t_{im}/2$$

denotes the relative probability that candidate c_i will tie for first place, given that there is a tie. By relative probability, I mean that $\Sigma\, t_i = 1$; it is for this reason that the divisor 2 is used, since each tie, by assumption, involves exactly two candidates.

[3] Voting for those candidates for whom $S(c_i) > 0$ is equivalent to voting for those for whom

$$u_i > \sum_{j=1}^{K} (t_{ij}/2t_i)\, u_j.$$

drops off if the voter casts either two few or too many votes. In chapter 7, I will return to the question of how many candidates to vote for under approval voting and, in particular, of the possible optimality of bullet-voting or plunking (voting for only one candidate).

It should be noted that implementation of the optimal strategy is qualitatively different and more difficult for the voter to follow under single-vote plurality than under approval voting. In particular, the voter's decision under approval voting requires only that, for each $i = 1, \ldots, K$, she expresses a preference between candidate c_i and a lottery involving the other candidates (see note 3 above). The weights of this lottery are related (but not exactly proportional) to the expected electoral strengths of the candidates.

On the other hand, the optimal decision for single-vote plurality voting requires that the voter attach a numerical quantity to her intensity of preference between candidate c_i and the lottery mentioned above, that she multiply that quantity by a measure of expected electoral strength, and then that she choose that candidate for whom this product is maximal (see note 2 above). Thus it seems likely that a loss of voting power for the individual due to deviation from the optimal strategy through ignorance or misunderstanding of that strategy may be more severe under single-vote plurality voting than it would be under approval voting.

Optimal strategies for the Borda count can also be obtained from this model.[4] Using Theorem 5.2 it is not hard to see that a voter's optimal strategy under the Borda count is to rank the candidates in the order determined by their strategic values $S(c_i)$. Note that this requires the same assignment of numerical quantities to intensities of preference and further calculations, as in the case of single-vote plurality. In the example above, the rational voter should rank the candidates in the order c_2, c_1, c_3, yielding an expected utility of 0.834, slightly higher than the corresponding value of 0.792 for the sincere ranking c_1, c_2, c_3.

---

[4] A modification of the Borda count called the adjusted Borda count (see D. Black 1958) yields the same optimal strategies. An expression of indifference between two or more candidates is permitted in the adjusted Borda method by allowing the voter to give the same rank to each candidate in the indifference group. For example, in a three-candidate election, a voter indifferent between the bottom two candidates could assign scores of 2, 0.5, and 0.5 instead of 2, 1, and 0. This is not permitted in the (unadjusted) Borda method. Alternatively, under the adjusted Borda method, the voter's score for each candidate can be defined as the number of candidates ranked strictly below that candidate minus the number ranked strictly above. Applied to the (unadjusted) Borda count, this rule provides scores which differ from the ordinary assignment of the values $K - 1, K - 2, \ldots, 0$ only by a linear transformation.

The following theorem summarizes the results concerning optimal strategies for plurality voting systems:

THEOREM 5.3. In a K-candidate race, the optimal strategies under risk using the criterion of expected utility are:

(a) Single-vote plurality: Vote for the candidate for whom $S(c_i)$
                                           is largest.

(b) Borda: Rank the candidates in order of the
                                           values of $S(c_i)$.

(c) Approval: Vote for c_i if and only if $S(c_i) > 0$.

As we have seen, $S(c_1)$ need not be the largest, nor $S(c_K)$ the smallest, strategic value. Thus optimal strategies under the single-vote plurality and Borda count systems need not be sincere. For approval voting, optimal strategies are sincere for three candidates, but not necessarily for more than three candidates (see also Brams and Fishburn 1978, 1983). Approval voting is, however, at least as sincere as the Borda count. To understand this, note that any insincere optimal strategy under approval voting implies that there exists some i and j such that $u_i > u_j$, but $S(c_i) < 0$ and $S(c_j) > 0$. But it follows then that $S(c_i) < S(c_j)$ so that the optimal strategy under the Borda count must rank c_j ahead of c_i. Such a strategy is insincere. The likelihood of insincere voting under various voting systems will be further pursued in chapters 6 and 7.

The nature of optimal strategies, under risk, for both cumulative voting and cardinal-measure voting are revealing. Under cumulative voting, the voter maximizes the expected utility of her vote by assigning all of her votes to the candidate possessing the highest strategic value $S(c_i)$. A shift of any votes from this strategy reduces the expected utility, according to Theorem 5.2. This result suggests that the opportunity under cumulative voting for the voter to spread her support over more than one candidate is of no value.

Under cardinal-measure voting, criterion (5.2) implies that a voter increases her expected utility by increasing her vote v_i for any candidate whose strategic value $S(c_i)$ exceeds 0 and by decreasing her vote for any candidate for whom $S(c_i)$ is less than 0. Hence the optimal strategy is to give the maximum allowed vote to any candidate for whom $S(c_i) > 0$ and the minimum permitted vote if $S(c_i) < 0$. In other words, the optimal strategy entails using only the extremes of the interval scale. The relation of cumulative and cardinal-measure voting to single-vote plurality and approval voting, respectively, will be considered in chapter 9, as well as a modification of cardinal-measure voting for which the full scale can be used in optimal voting.

5.5. A SIMPLIFIED CRITERION FOR DECISIONS UNDER RISK

As an approximation, I suppose that there exist numbers p_i, $i = 1, \ldots, K$, with $\Sigma p_i = 1$, such that the quantities t_{ij} are proportional to the product of the quantities p_i and p_j. The t_{ij} represent, as before, the conditional probabilities, given that there is a tie for first place, that the pair of candidates tying are c_i and c_j. For approval voting, this leads to a substantial simplification of the optimal strategy for voting under risk. In fact, the criterion given by $S(c_i) > 0$, holds if and only if[5]

$$u_i > \sum_{j=1}^{K} p_j u_j. \tag{5.4}$$

To interpret criterion (5.4), define t_j as the relative probability, given that there is a tie, that the jth candidate ties for first place (see note 2, above, where it is noted that $\Sigma t_j = 1$). A little algebra[6] shows that, very roughly, (5.4) can be replaced by the rule of thumb

$$u_i > \sum_{j=1}^{K} t_j u_j. \tag{5.5}$$

Fortunately, formula (5.5), although derived by a circuitous sequence of approximations, has a direct intuitive interpretation. Given that there is a tie for first place, before the focal voter votes, t_j denotes the relative probability that the tie involves candidate c_j. The voter has an incentive to vote

[5] The supposition above is equivalent to assuming that there is a constant k such that $t_{ij} = kp_i p_j (i \neq j)$ and $t_{ii} = 0$. Thus

$$S(c_i) = \sum_{j=1}^{K} (u_i - u_j) t_{ij} = kp_i \sum_{j=1}^{K} (u_i - u_j) p_j.$$

It follows that $S(c_i) > 0$ if and only if

$$\sum_{j=1}^{K} (u_i - u_j) p_j > 0,$$

which is equivalent to (5.4).

[6] The ratio $t_j/p_j = (k/2)(1 - p_j)$. Since $\Sigma t_j = \Sigma p_j = 1$, if all p_j are small so that $(1 - p_j)$ are nearly constant over j, this implies that p_j very roughly approximates t_j, so that (5.5) is approximately true when (5.4) is true.

for any candidate whose utility exceeds the expected utility $\Sigma\, t_j u_j$ of a candidate in the tie.

In the example described in section 5.4, $t_1 = 3/12$, $t_2 = 5/12$, and $t_3 = 4/12$, reflecting the fact that the focal voter rates the strengths of the candidates in the order c_2, c_3, c_1. It follows that the cutpoint $\Sigma\, t_j u_j = (3/12) \times 1 + (5/12) \times (3/4) + (4/12) \times 0 = 0.562$, suggesting that the rational approval voter should vote for both candidates (c_1 and c_2) whose utilities exceed the value 0.562.

Thus, the approval voter must compare the utility for candidate c_i with a weighted average of the utilities for the other candidates. For each c_i she must express a preference between candidate c_i on the one hand and a von Neumann–Morgenstern lottery involving the other candidates on the other. That is to say, the voter has the option of taking candidate c_i for certain or a gamble in which one of the others is chosen with certain probabilities.

Note that under approval voting, a strategy defined by (5.5) is always sincere. This follows since the quantity $\Sigma\, t_j u_j$ is independent of i. Thus no candidate voted for in the strategy may receive a utility u_i less than that of a candidate for whom the voter did not vote.[7] In effect, in my simplification of the model, I have replaced the requirement that the voter estimate the relative likelihoods that pairs of candidates tie for first place with the easier and more natural requirement that she estimate the relative likelihoods that individual candidates may tie for first place.

A further modification may be obtained by relating the t_j to the probability of winning. Suppose that we denote by w_j the probability that the jth candidate win in the judgment of the focal voter. Tideman has suggested that t_j is proportional to $\sqrt{w_j}$.[8] Under this assumption, (5.5) is replaced by

[7] If, however, the t_{ij} are not proportional to a product $p_i p_j$, insincere optimal strategies may be constructed for elections with four or more candidates. Detailed analysis for four-candidate elections suggests that the likelihood of insincere optimal strategies may be very low and the distinctions involved implausible for a voter to carry out (see Hoffman 1982; and Carter 1987). For this reason, Carter argues that approval voting strategies that skip down the preference order should not be considered admissible in practice. In any event, regardless of the number of candidates, it is always optimal under approval voting to vote for one's first choice and not to vote for one's last choice.

[8] I am indebted to Nicolaus Tideman for suggesting the use of the square root and the following motivation for its use. For three candidates, the possible outcomes of an election may be modeled as the triangle in the positive orthant of three-dimensional space whose coordinates sum to the number of votes cast. The winner is the candidate whose vertex is closest to the outcome. The w_j are subjective masses of probability assigned to the thirds of the triangle closest to the three vertices, respectively. The probability that one's vote will be decisive between a pair of candidates is equal to the probability mass in a narrow rectangle around the border between the regions assigned to the two candidates. The mass of each rectangle should be in proportion to an average of the neighboring w_js. A geometric average, $\sqrt{w_i w_j}$,

$$u_i > (1/w) \sum_{j=1}^{K} \sqrt{w_j} u_j \qquad (5.6)$$

where $w = \Sigma \sqrt{w_j}$. This requires the voter to compare the utility of the ith candidate with a weighted average of the utilities of the other candidates, where the weights are related to the likelihood of winning.

5.6. DISCUSSION AND CONCLUSIONS

Under the single-vote plurality and Borda count systems, an optimal strategy under risk requires the voter, as we have seen, to rank the quantities $S(c_i)$ (at least partially for single-vote plurality voting and completely for the Borda count). It would appear both difficult and distracting for even a sophisticated voter to discover her optimal strategy making these calculations, let alone for the typical voter. In contrast, under approval voting, the voter need only express a preference between each candidate and a lottery involving the other candidates.

If the voter has little knowledge of the likely outcome of the election, she might assume equiprobable outcomes as a working hypothesis. Maximizing expected utility under this assumption is mathematically equivalent to using the Laplace method (for decisions under uncertainty) and leads to sincere voting for the single-vote plurality, Borda count, and approval systems. In particular, the optimal strategy under approval voting is to vote for those candidates rated above the (simple) average of the utilities of all candidates. This should be compared to the Savage regret optimal strategy of voting for all candidates rated above the average of the utilities of the most and least preferred candidates.

If the utilities u_i are symmetrically distributed, a typical optimal strategy under approval voting would involve voting for about half the candidates. In chapter 7, we will consider empirical evidence that a voter's utilities u_i are unlikely to be symmetrically distributed, but rather that the higher utilities may be more spaced out, while the lower utilities may be more bunched, i.e., the distribution may be negatively skewed.

Such an asymmetrical distribution of utilities implies that typically less than half the candidates will fall above the mean utility. As we will see in chapter 7, this effect is accentuated by unequal weights t_i that are likely if knowledge of the strengths of candidates is available. The resultant expectation that a voter optimally vote for less than half of the candidates ap-

---

is attractive because it corresponds to assuming smooth exponential growth between a relative probability of w_i at the center of the region adjacent to c_i and a relative probability of w_j at the center of the region adjacent to c_j.

pears born out empirically in a number of approval balloting polls (see chapter 7).

In any event, if voters are repeatedly forced to make approval voting decisions in actual elections, they may be better able to approximate their optimal strategies than when they are first presented with an approval voting ballot or poll. Evidence relating to this conjecture awaits repeated trials of approval voting.

6

....

STRATEGIC VOTING

AND ITS EFFECTS ON

CONDORCET EFFICIENCY

6.1. INTRODUCTION

Information gathered through polls or other sources fuels strategic voting in a variety of ways, depending on the electoral procedure in use. This chapter investigates such strategies and their impact on Condorcet efficiency for each of the voting systems introduced in chapter 1. The results suggest a major reassessment of the relative merits of these procedures in meeting the Condorcet criterion.

Three sets of assumptions are considered: (1) those suggested by Brams (1982, 1983) for single-vote plurality and for approval voting and natural analogues of these assumptions for other systems, (2) strategic voting based on the proportions of votes received in polls (for plurality voting systems only), and (3) sophisticated voting as defined by Farquharson (1969). The consequences of Brams's assumptions are explored in section 6.2. Simulation techniques, using assumptions (2) and (3), are employed in sections 6.3 and 6.4 to further measure the effect of strategic voting for the three plurality systems: single-vote plurality, the Borda count, and approval voting. This analysis substantiates the more general arguments given in section 6.2. Similar analysis indicates that the effect of strategic voting on social-utility efficiency mimics its effect on Condorcet efficiency. For this reason, only a brief discussion of social utility is given.

Empirical analysis of Condorcet efficiency and strategic voting, based on inferences from polling data and on balloting in a large private organization, are presented in sections 6.5 and 6.6. Worst-case estimates of the costs of sincere voting are considered in section 6.7.

6.2. EFFECTS OF BRAMS'S POLL ASSUMPTIONS ON CONDORCET EFFICIENCY

Brams (1982; 1983, ch. 7) assumes that under single-vote plurality or approval voting systems, voters use a poll (conducted under the respective system) to identify the top two candidates. Under either system, the voter votes for his preference between these two. Under approval voting, if his sincere ballot includes exactly one of the two front-runners, it remains unchanged after the poll; otherwise, in addition to voting for his preference between the top two, he votes for all candidates preferred to this candidate. To extend this idea to Borda voting, I assume that the voter, in order to widen the gap between the two front-runners, ranks the top two candidates identified by the poll first and last, respectively, using the intermediate ranks for the others in the order of his true preferences.

Extension of the Brams concept to elimination methods depends on the type of poll. Such a poll could (1) report only the number of first preferences for each candidate, or, more ambitiously (2) gather preference profiles from respondents and use them to apply the appropriate elimination procedure. Presumably in the latter case the order of elimination rather than numerical scores would be reported.

Under the Hare (or single-transferable-vote) system, the first type of poll simply identifies the two (first-preference) front-runners. If, after the poll, all voters report one or the other of these as first preference, one of them receives a majority and is elected. Thus, assuming the poll constitutes a faithful sample of the electorate, the combination of a poll followed by a Hare ballot acts like a runoff. The second type of poll might induce voters to choose between the last two candidates to remain in the elimination contest. Hence, the effect of a Hare ballot with such a poll is the same as without it. In either case, the Condorcet efficiency is unlikely to be affected significantly by the poll, because the Hare and runoff systems have comparable Condorcet efficiencies.

In fact, restricting first-preference votes to front-runners, although it may be intuitively appealing to some voters, is not likely to be optimal. A first preference for an expected trailer might help him win, but if it doesn't, the vote can be transferred to a candidate of lower preference who survives longer in the elimination contest. There is, thus, no inherent penalty for awarding a first preference to a trailer.

There is also no incentive, as there is under the Borda count, for a voter to move the chief rival of his favorite to the bottom of his preference order. As long as his favorite remains in the race, lower preferences are not counted. If his favorite is eliminated, there is no motivation for the voter to try to punish his former chief rival. Indeed, since the Hare system appears very difficult to manipulate (see section 6.6), strategic voting tends to be identical with sincere voting, so that Condorcet efficiency is little affected.

Under the runoff system and a poll of type one, the voters' attention would be restricted to the top two vote-getters, exactly as would occur anyway (assuming that the poll is faithful) on the second ballot, so that no substantial effect on Condorcet efficiency should be expected. A poll of the second type—again assuming a faithful poll—simply makes the first ballot redundant.

When the Coombs procedure is used, a natural extension of the Brams rule would specify that a voter would give first preference to his preferred front-runner and last preference to the other front-runner (as under the Borda count) in order to try to eliminate the favorite's chief rival at an early stage. If this occurs, the two front-runners will share all the last preferences, so one of them will be the first to be eliminated and the other is likely to be next. For a poll of type two, the very tendency of the Coombs system—in the absence of strategic voting—to choose the Condorcet candidate implies that, following a poll that identifies the last two survivors, the Coombs system is highly likely to defeat the Condorcet candidate. The ambiguity of a poll of type one might, on the other hand, permit a Condorcet winner to emerge slightly more often, but only when that candidate ranked third or lower in first preferences. Even if a poll is conducted reporting only last preferences, it would reveal likely front-runners (candidates with few last preferences), again inviting voters to manipulate.

Thus, among elimination procedures, the Condorcet efficiency of the Hare and runoff methods would appear to be little affected by polling information, whereas that of the Coombs system would likely drop disastrously.

The effects and implications of poll reporting under the Black or other Condorcet completion methods seem less clear. However the two front-runners are identified, voters would likely respond with first and last preferences for these two, as under the Borda and Coombs systems. Assuming that voters follow this rule blindly, the front-runner receiving a majority of these poll-induced first preferences would likely be the true Condorcet candidate. This result appears unstable, however, when defections from the rule are permitted. For example, suppose there are nine voters with the following preference orders:

4 voters	4 voters	1 voter
A	B	C
B	A	A
C	C	B

Any reasonable poll will identify A and B as the front-runners, leading to the following reported preferences under our extension of the Brams rule:

4 voters	4 voters	1 voter
A	B	A
C	C	C
B	A	B

Now A (the true Condorcet candidate) is elected as the poll-induced Condorcet winner. If, however, the one voter who truly prefers C keeps C in first place, C becomes the poll-induced Condorcet winner, despite being beaten 8 to 1 by both A and B among true preferences.

Since the poll-induced strategies described above will typically elevate trailing candidates to intermediate preferences while demoting front-runners to many last-place preferences, this unfortunate result is not just an artifact of a contrived example. We are forced to conclude that, under the curse of knowledge, even a Condorcet completion method need not elect the Condorcet candidate even if there is one!

By contrast, a poll under the single-vote plurality system induces the voter, according to the Brams rule, to vote for his preference between two front-runners. The effect would appear similar to a runoff, except that the first ballot is actually a poll. Since the runoff method yields a higher Condorcet efficiency than does single-vote plurality, a poll should make the latter system more Condorcet efficient.

Under approval voting, the Brams rule requires everyone to vote for one of two front-runners. With this advantage, one of them is almost certain to win. Thus a poll followed by an approval ballot resembles an approval ballot with a runoff. In fact, the poll-ballot combination has the advantage that poll respondents would seem to be unlikely to report strategically—by, for example, naming a pushover—as they might on an official ballot. Since a runoff tends to increase Condorcet efficiency, we would expect that efficiency to increase for both single-vote plurality and approval voting when preceded by a poll.

6.3. SIMULATION RESULTS FOR PLURALITY VOTING SYSTEMS

Simulation findings substantiate the effects of strategic voting on Condorcet efficiency suggested by the arguments in section 6.2. Table 6.1 presents the results of six hundred simulated elections for the three plurality voting systems.[1]

---

[1] Each run involved four candidates, using a spatial model with four dimensions, each pair of variates having correlation 0.5, and the relative dispersion (RD) = 1.

TABLE 6.1. Condorcet Efficiencies with Polling Information under
Brams's Assumptions

System	Sincere voting	After poll 1	After poll 2
Single-vote plurality	72	93	93
Approval	85	99+	99
Borda	91	71	87

SOURCE: S. Merrill, "A Statistical Model for Condorcet Efficiency Based on Simulation under Spatial Model Assumptions," *Public Choice* 47 (1985): 398, Table 4; adapted with permission.

Under these assumptions, Condorcet efficiency for single-vote plurality and approval voting increase sharply with the first poll, as expected, and stabilize thereafter. By contrast, for the Borda count, Condorcet efficiency drops markedly following the first poll, then rises again with the second. This phenomenon is easily explained. After the first poll, the two strongest candidates share the first and last ranks, giving each a roughly average Borda count. The other candidates receive intermediate ranks, so their Borda counts too do not deviate greatly from the average. The collective ranking of the resulting tight contest is statistically unstable. But this very randomness prevents the victimization of strong candidates after the second poll, leading to a rebound in Condorcet efficiency. Simulation results indicate a similar pattern of changes in social-utility efficiency as a result of Brams's strategic assumptions for the three plurality methods.

Alternatively, I assume that voters react continuously (not discretely) to vote totals as reported in polls. In section 5.5, a simplified formula was obtained for the strategic value of the ith candidate $S(c_i)$ under the assumption that the t_{ij} are approximately proportional to $t_i t_j$, the product of the respective relative probabilities that candidates c_i and c_j tie for first place, given that there is a tie. In that section, the formula is further modified, taking t_j proportional to $\sqrt{w_j}$, where w_j is the probability that the jth candidate will win.

To operationalize these quantities, set w_j proportional to a power of the proportion p_j of the vote received (in the poll) by candidate c_j. A power greater than 1 seems appropriate, since a plot of w_j versus the proportion of the vote should have positive second derivative, i.e., the likelihood that a candidate wins increases more rapidly as his proportion of the vote approaches 50 percent. I have used a square, admittedly in part because it simplifies (5.3), yielding

$$S(c_i) = K \sum_{j=1}^{K} p_i p_j (u_i - u_j).$$

Using optimal strategies, simulation results for a four-dimensional model, with pairwise correlation $= 0.5$, $RD = 1$, and one thousand elections, are given in table 6.2. The results are similar to those following Brams's assumptions, except that the continuous shading of strategies eliminates the wild oscillations that occur under the Borda count.

6.4. SIMULATIONS FOR SOPHISTICATED VOTING

Other studies using different assumptions have arrived at similar substantive conclusions. Felsenthal, Maoz, and Rapoport (1985) investigate, by computer simulation, the Condorcet efficiency of single-vote plurality and approval voting under both sincere and sophisticated voting.

Their definition of sophisticated voting follows Farquharson (1969), i.e., all voters are assumed to have complete knowledge of others' preference orders, to vote in blocs according to preference order, to fail to cooperate with voters having different preference orders, and to employ only admissible (undominated) strategies (see Glossary). Farquharson assumes each voter successively eliminates inadmissible strategies until such elimination is no longer possible.

TABLE 6.2. Condorcet Efficiencies with Polling Information Using Optimal Strategies under Risk

System	K = 3			K = 5		
	Sincere voting	After poll 1	After poll 2	Sincere voting	After poll 1	After poll 2
Single-vote plurality	84	89	91	68	74	77
Approval	88	97	97	77	87	88
Borda	93	94	92	88	87	85

SOURCE: S. Merrill, "A Statistical Model for Condorcet Efficiency Based on Simulation under Spatial Model Assumptions," *Public Choice* 47 (1985): 400, Table 5; adapted with permission.

Felsenthal et al. further assume that all voters have strict preference orders and that all permutations of preference orders and size relationships among relevant groups of voters are equally likely. Because of the complexity of these conditions and of the procedures to determine sophisticated voting, their analysis is limited to three candidates and to no more than five blocs of voters.

These authors conclude that (a) "approval voting is significantly more Condorcet-efficient than [single-vote] plurality voting" and (b) "sophisticated voting, under both procedures, seems to be more Condorcet-efficient than sincere voting." Although the assumption that all blocs and size relationships are equally likely is somewhat restrictive, the results appear to confirm those presented above based on expected utility analysis.

6.5. INFERENCES FROM POLLING DATA

This section deals with the effect that alternative voting systems might have had on the outcome of historical elections, assessing the relationship between Condorcet efficiency and strategic voting. The studies reported infer likely voting behavior by interpreting as utilities, u_i, the "thermometer" ratings[2] by respondents for candidates in the American National Election Studies conducted by the Center for Political Studies.

Tideman (1981) studied the Condorcet efficiency and the resistance to strategic voting of the single-vote plurality, Borda, Hare, and Black systems, as well as a Condorcet completion method adapted from Dodgson (Lewis Carroll), which selects, in the absence of a Condorcet candidate, that candidate who would become the Condorcet candidate by changing the fewest ballots. He formed 924 putative elections from triples of candidates included in the 1972 and 1976 American National Election Studies, using thermometer ratings as utilities.

Tideman found Condorcet efficiency uniformly much higher than it would be for an impartial culture. For example, the efficiency for single-vote plurality rises from 79% for either an impartial culture or a typical spatial model[3] to 95% in Tideman's study. The rankings of voting procedures with regard to Condorcet efficiency are, however, the same as those obtained by most simulation scenarios, using either an impartial culture (table 2.1) or a spatial model (table 2.2). To assess manipulability, Tideman (1981) measured the (harmonic) mean of the fraction of the electorate required to manipulate the outcome. The Borda count and the single-vote

---

[2] "Thermometer" scores are ratings of candidates on a scale from 0 to 100 elicited from voters on the basis of "warmth" for each candidate.

[3] The spatial model (for three candidates) specified two dimensions with correlation = 0.5 and relative dispersion = 1.0.

plurality systems were found by this measure to be the most manipulable, whereas the Hare and Dodgson systems were found to be the least manip- ulable (see also the analysis in section 6.6).

An alternative analysis, also employing thermometer scores, assumes optimal strategies under the criterion of expected utility for equiprobable outcomes (i.e., under the Laplace criterion—see section 5.2). Merrill (1981) used this criterion in two hypothetical contests employing 1,017 respondents classified as "strong" or "weak" Democrats in the 1972 American National Election Study. The first race included only the four Democratic candidates most active in the primaries: Hubert Humphrey, George McGovern, Edmund Muskie, and George Wallace. The second in- cluded also Shirley Chisholm, Thomas Eagleton, Henry Jackson, Edward Kennedy, John Lindsay, and Sargent Shriver, which together with the four in the first race constituted all ten Democrats covered in the survey. In the second race, the number of usable respondents dropped to 998.

The three plurality voting systems were considered: single-vote plural- ity, Borda, and approval voting. In each case, the total vote received was divided by the number of respondents and then multiplied by 100 to rep- resent a percentage of the maximal vote possible for a single candidate for that system. In the case of the Borda count, the vote totals were further divided by $K - 1$, because that is the highest vote a voter can assign to a candidate. This placed the results for each system on an equal footing for easy comparison. Also included was the mean or social-utility (range-nor- malized thermometer score) for each candidate. The results are presented in table 6.3.

Note that the results of the Borda count and approval voting are quite similar to each other and to the mean utilities. In the four-candidate race, all lead to a Humphrey, McGovern, Muskie, Wallace finish. Humphrey, furthermore, is the Condorcet candidate. However, the single-vote plural- ity method elevates McGovern to first place and drops Muskie to a weak fourth. For the ten-candidate race, the order of finish for the top six can- didates is identical for Borda, approval voting, and mean utility. But, al- though Wallace finishes second under single-vote plurality, he drops to seventh or lower under the alternative systems. On the other hand, Hum- phrey—fourth under single-vote plurality—is second under each of the other procedures. Earlier analysis of the same data set on a state-by-state basis by Joslyn (1976) suggests that the runoff and Hare systems also pro- duce results similar to those of the Borda count and the Condorcet crite- rion, but dissimilar to that of single-vote plurality.

Table 6.4 presents an analysis of the same race using strategic voting un- der risk. As in section 5.5, let t_j denote the voter's subjective relative prob- ability that candidate c_j will tie for first place, given that there is a tie. As-

TABLE 6.3. Expected Vote Using Optimal Strategies for Equiprobable
Outcomes for 1972 Democratic Candidates

(a) Four-candidate race

Candidate	Single-vote plurality	Borda	Approval	Mean utility
Humphrey	29	60	64	63
McGovern	33	57	58	59
Muskie	13	44	45	47
Wallace	25	38	36	38

(b) Ten-candidate race

Candidate	Single-vote plurality	Borda	Approval	Mean utility
Kennedy	29	68	71	69
Humphrey	12	61	67	61
McGovern	14	58	61	58
Shriver	6	55	59	56
Eagleton	5	50	48	50
Muskie	5	48	44	49
Jackson	3	39	31	41
Lindsay	2	40	33	41
Wallace	19	42	40	40
Chisholm	4	39	35	39

sume that voters under approval voting vote for each candidate c_i whose
utility u_i exceeds the average utility of all candidates, weighted by the t_j, as
specified in formula (5.5). In the scenario in table 6.4, the values of the
weights, t_j, for Humphrey, McGovern, Muskie, and Wallace were chosen
proportional to 4, 4, 1, and 2, respectively.[4]

The assumption of strategic voting has little effect on the results of

[4] The values of t_j for this scenario were selected with single-vote plurality in mind. For the
Borda count or approval voting, it might be more realistic to reverse the t_j for Muskie and
Wallace. That change was found to have little effect on the Borda and approval vote totals.

TABLE 6.4. Expected Votes Using Strategic Voting under Risk for
1972 Democratic Candidates

Candidate	t_j	Single-vote plurality	Borda	Approval	Mean utility
Humphrey	4	38	60	62	63
McGovern	4	39	56	56	59
Muskie	1	3	46	41	47
Wallace	2	20	38	36	38

Borda and approval voting for this election. Under single-vote plurality, however, the totals for Wallace and especially those for Muskie drop as voters desert them to avoid "wasting their votes."

As a measure of the effect of new entrants on the relative standings of previous candidates under alternative voting systems, one may compare the order of finish of the four most active candidates in the two races reported in table 6.3 (see also section 9.2). For the Borda count and approval voting, the introduction of six new candidates leaves the order of finish of the original four unchanged. Under single-vote plurality, however, the order changes from McGovern–Humphrey–Wallace–Muskie to Wallace–McGovern–Humphrey–Muskie. In the ten-candidate race, Wallace finishes second (behind Kennedy) under the single-vote plurality method, but from sixth to tenth under the other rules.

6.6. EMPIRICAL EVIDENCE FROM PRESIDENTIAL ELECTIONS OF THE AMERICAN PSYCHOLOGICAL ASSOCIATION

The American Psychological Association (APA), because of the size and diversity of its membership, the competitiveness of its presidential elections, and the significance of its presidential role in representing the society to the public and to Congress, shares many characteristics with public elections. The association, furthermore, uses the Hare system to select its president each year from a slate of five nominees, requiring each voter to rank the candidates.

For these reasons, the perceptive study by Chamberlin, Cohen, and Coombs (1984) of five APA presidential elections (1976, 1978, 1979, 1980, 1981) involving numbers of voters ranging from 11,000 to 15,000 provide valuable insight into the effects of real preference structures on

73

Condorcet efficiency and the manipulability of voting systems. Not only was there a Condorcet candidate in each of the five elections, but in each case there was a complete transitive majority ordering, i.e., an ordering of candidates A, B, C, D, and E such that (the Condorcet candidate) A beats B, B beats C, C beats D, and D beats E. As we have seen, such a result is to be expected in a spatial model, but not in an impartial culture.[5]

Chamberlin et al. consider five of the seven voting systems discussed here: single-vote plurality, Borda, Hare, Coombs, and approval voting.[6] In each case, sincere voting is assumed, with each approval voter casting a ballot for exactly two of the five candidates.[7] Single-vote plurality fails to choose the Condorcet candidate in two elections out of five; in a third election, the Condorcet candidate is tied for first place. The Borda count and approval voting fail once each. The Hare and Coombs methods always choose the Condorcet candidate.

The distance between the majority ordering and that ordering determined by a voting system[8] varies with the voting system in a way that does not reflect Condorcet efficiency. The largest average distance occurs for the Coombs method and the smallest for Borda and approval voting. Complete results are given in table 6.5. These findings suggest that the elimination methods, although they are efficient in choosing the Condorcet candidate, may not be effective in achieving a majority ranking.

To assess manipulability, Chamberlin et al. determined for each voting system the minimum coalition size needed to subvert the sincere winner, expressed as a percentage of the voters with the incentive and the ability to aid in manipulation, if such subversion is possible. The most striking conclusion, as indicated in table 6.5, is the lack of susceptibility to subversion of the Hare system, a finding in agreement with Tideman's inferences from polling data on U.S. presidential candidates (see section 6.5).

Further empirical analysis of the proportion of elections that are manipulable is given in Chamberlin and Featherston (1986). Based on one thousand electorates simulated to resemble preference profiles observed in the APA presidential balloting, they found almost all elections manipulable for

[5] Under an impartial culture, the probability that at least one of five elections will fail to have a Condorcet candidate is 0.75 (see, e.g., Gehrlein 1983).

[6] Incomplete ballot rankings were completed randomly. Chamberlin et al. also present an alternative ballot completion method in which completed rankings were assigned in the proportion for which these rankings occurred among complete ballots whose initial sections agreed with the truncated ballots. The results are different, but they do not substantially alter the thrust of the findings presented here.

[7] The assumption that approval voters cast a ballot for two out of five candidates is consonant with the optimal strategies obtained from the analysis in chapter 7.

[8] Distance is defined as the number of adjacent pairs of candidates that must be permuted to change the ordering generated by one of the voting methods into the majority ordering.

TABLE 6.5. Condorcet Efficiency and Manipulability in
the APA Presidential Elections

System	Condorcet efficiency	Distance[a]	Manipulability[b]
Single-vote plurality	50	1.0	12.8
Borda	80	0.2	4.5
Hare	100	0.8	[c]
Coombs	100	1.2	5.7
Approval voting	80	0.2	8.3

SOURCE: J. R. Chamberlin, J. L. Cohen, and C. H. Coombs, "Social Choice Observed: Five Presidential Elections of the American Psychological Association," *Journal of Politics* 46 (1984): 479–502, Tables 2, 3, and 7; adapted with permission.

[a] Mean distance from majority ordering.

[b] Mean minimum coalition size as a percentage of voters with the incentive and ability to aid in manipulation.

[c] The Hare system was manipulable in only one of the five elections, in which the minimum percent was 0.7.

the single-vote plurality, Borda, and Coombs systems, but only about 25 percent manipulable under the Hare procedure. Chamberlin and Featherston further found that Condorcet efficiencies for these elections (both real and simulated) were comparable to the values obtained in chapter 2.

Recall that manipulation for single-vote plurality takes the form of the desertion of trailers. For the Borda and Coombs methods, the standard strategy is to rank the chief rival of one's favorite last. For approval voting, it usually consists of the weakly insincere act of truncation or the expansion of one's ballot (see chapter 7).

Under the Hare system, manipulation on behalf of a candidate normally involves throwing some (but not too much) of the candidate's support to a pushover, who may thereby eliminate a chief rival at an early stage. Such a strategy requires a quantitative estimate of the amount of support to be shifted as well as an awkward exhortation to supporters to give first preference to another candidate in order to help their favorite. This strategy, if it is possible at all, is at once difficult to design and implausible to implement in a large electorate.

Manipulation of the Hare system thus often involves exploiting the fact that it violates the monotonicity condition (see Doron and Kronick 1977, or section 9.2 for examples). This condition states that if some voters lower (or raise) a certain candidate's position in their ranking orders while all other preferences remain constant, then the voting system should not raise (or lower) that candidate in the social ranking. Although this is a serious theoretical defect (see Fishburn and Brams 1983), its use as a means of manipulation appears unlikely in practice, particularly for large electorates.

6.7. THE COSTS OF SINCERE VOTING

The inducements for voters to use strategic voting under various electoral systems can be investigated by measuring the costs of sincere voting. Such a study was conducted by Hoffman (1983), who defines for each voting system the *efficiency of sincere voting* as the ratio of the maximum utility achievable through a sincere ballot to the maximum attainable through any permissible ballot.

For three candidates, Hoffman proved the worst-case efficiencies of sincere voting to be 0 for single-vote plurality and the Hare system, 0.5 for the Borda count, and 1.0 for approval voting. Efficiencies for more than three candidates are presented in table 6.6.

These results suggest that approval voting may induce sincere voting by incurring smaller costs than other systems. It should be remembered, however, that these are worst-case results. Estimates of the average cost, defined in an appropriate sense, would be useful.

TABLE 6.6. Efficiency of Sincere Voting

| System | Number of candidates | | | |
	3	4	5	K
Single-vote plurality	0	0	0	0
Hare	0	0	0	0
Borda	1/2	1/3	1/4	$1/(K-1)$
Approval voting	1	1/2[a]	1/2[a]	$1/[K/2]$[a]

SOURCE: D. Hoffman, "Relative Efficiency of Voting Systems," *SIAM Journal of Applied Mathematics* 43 (1983): 1218, Table 1; adapted with permission of the Society for Industrial and Applied Mathematics. All rights reserved. Copyright 1983 by the Society for Industrial and Applied Mathematics.

[a] Any value designated by [a] is a lower bound: the exact efficiency has not been determined and may be higher. The symbol [x] means the largest integer less than or equal to x.

6.8. CONCLUSIONS

The implications for Condorcet efficiency of each of several possible assumptions about the strategic reaction to polling knowledge—Brams's rules, the optimization of expected utility, and sophisticated voting—are all consistent insofar as they are comparable:

CONCLUSION 1. *Strategic response to preelection polls tends to increase the Condorcet efficiency of the single-vote plurality and approval voting systems, primarily by focusing voter attention on the front-runners.*

Effectively, this strategy reduces the number of candidates in the race, making the choice of the Condorcet candidate more likely. If, however, the Condorcet candidate is third or worse in the poll—a common occurrence under single-vote plurality—the likelihood of his selection is decreased by strategic voting.

The favorable effects of strategic voting on Condorcet efficiency for single-vote plurality and approval voting depend on assumptions that a poll accurately reflects the standings of the candidates, that the voters place confidence in the poll, and that they react to it strategically. Since all of these expectations are problematical, strategic improvement in Condorcet efficiency may be significantly less than predicted by simulation.

CONCLUSION 2. *The Condorcet efficiency of the Hare and runoff systems are relatively less affected by polling knowledge, since manipulation appears difficult to implement.*

CONCLUSION 3. *The Coombs and Borda count systems appear to invite manipulation as voters seek to separate front-runners as much as possible in their preference orders.*

The inference in Conclusion 2 is strongly supported by evidence from presidential elections of the American Psychological Association. The manipulation described in Conclusion 3 erodes a major portion of the non-first-preference support of the front-runners, one of whom is usually the Condorcet candidate. Curiously, even a Condorcet completion method, such as that of Black, can also place front-runners in a position vulnerable to manipulation, subverting the selection of the Condorcet candidate.

Worst-case estimates suggest that the cost of sincere voting—in terms of lost expected utility—is potentially higher for single-vote plurality and Hare than for approval voting. The Hare system, on the other hand, appears in empirical studies distinctly less manipulable than single-vote plurality or the Borda count and probably less so than approval voting.

To summarize, we have seen evidence that strategic response to polling

77

information would likely decrease the Condorcet efficiency of the Coombs, Borda, and Condorcet completion methods, whereas it would tend to increase that of single-vote plurality and approval voting. The Condorcet efficiency for the Hare and runoff systems would be little changed by polls. Coupling these results with the simulation data on Condorcet efficiency from chapters 2 and 4, the systems yielding the highest Condorcet efficiency in the face of strategic voting would appear to be approval voting, Hare, and runoff, probably in that order.

7

∎ ∎ ∎ ∎ ∎ ∎ ∎ ∎ ∎ ∎ ∎ ∎ ∎ ∎ ∎ ∎ ∎ ∎ ∎ ∎

STRATEGIC VOTING FOR

APPROVAL BALLOTING UNDER

ALTERNATIVE DECISION RULES

7.1. Introduction

The increased flexibility offered by approval voting suggests that a more differentiated view of sincerity would be useful in assessing the strategic options available. In the following sections we introduce such a perspective and use it to study not only the usual approval voting system (with the plurality decision rule), but also approval balloting coupled with alternative decision rules, especially two-stage rules. Much of this chapter is based on the work of Merrill and Nagel (1987).

Under approval balloting, the voter must decide not only for whom to vote but also for how many candidates to vote. The five levels of sincerity introduced by Merrill and Nagel (1987) and outlined in section 7.2 are intended to clarify normative judgments amid this greater strategic freedom. They are based on how an ingenuous citizen might vote, without knowledge of the likely votes of others.

7.2. Levels of Sincerity

The point of departure for specifying levels of sincerity under approval voting is the rule obtained by Merrill (1979), Weber (1977), and Brams and Fishburn (1983, 84–88) that a voter without knowledge of others' votes maximizes her expected utility by voting for every candidate whose utility for her exceeds the mean utility of all candidates. This criterion defines the first level of sincerity (pure sincerity); the others are obtained by successive modifications of this strategy. A voting strategy is said to *skip* if it includes a vote for any candidate, without also including a vote for all candidates strictly preferred to that candidate.

(a) *Pure sincerity*. A ballot for those candidates whose utilities u_i exceed the mean utility for all candidates.

(b) *Truncation*. A ballot for fewer candidates than prescribed by pure sincerity, but without a skip.

(c) *Expansion*. A ballot for more candidates than prescribed by pure sincerity, but without a skip.

(d) *Skipping*. Any strategy that involves a skip but includes a vote for one's first choice.

(e) *Decapitation*. A nonabstention that omits a vote for one's first choice.

If voter utilities u_i are symmetrically distributed, one would expect fifty percent on the average of the utilities to exceed the mean for each voter, suggesting that the strategy of pure sincerity would involve, on the average, voting for about half the candidates. However, if voter utilities are negatively skewed, i.e., more bunched toward the low end of the scale, fewer than half would be expected to exceed the mean.

The work of Snider (1979), who asked respondents to make psychophysical evaluations of candidates, suggests that utilities (for the voters he studied) are indeed negatively skewed. In fact, Snider found that a plot of utility against preference order was approximately in the shape of the curve $y = x^2$ (see also Appendix B). Thus, even without polling information, the pure sincerity optimal strategy prescribes, in general, voting for less than half of the candidates.

The introduction of polling information would appear to elevate the cut-point for determining the optimal strategy even more. Formula (5.5) where t_j denotes the relative probability that candidate c_j will tie for first place, given that there is a tie, indicates that the voter should vote for candidate c_i if

$$u_i > \sum_{j=1}^{K} t_j u_j. \tag{7.1}$$

Front-runners tend to have high utility for many voters (that is indirectly why they are front-runners). By definition, their values of t_j are also high. Hence the cut-point $\sum t_j u_j$ is weighted toward high utility, making the criterion specified by (7.1) more stringent, as voters take polling information into account. Intuitively, distinctions between front-runners are more important than other distinctions, so the cut-point is often placed between their (likely) high utilities. This suggests that deviations from pure sincerity are most likely to be in the direction of truncation.

For example, suppose that there are four candidates who, for some focal voter, have symmetrically distributed utilities: 10, 6, 4, and 0. Assume further that the weighing factors t_j that appear in (7.1) are 0.4, 0.4, 0.1, and 0.1, respectively, i.e., the first two are the front-runners. In this case, the weighted average in (7.1) is:

$$0.4 \times 10 + 0.4 \times 6 + 0.1 \times 4 + 0.1 \times 0 = 6.8.$$

It follows that only one candidate, the one rated 10, exceeds the cut-point and is the only candidate voted for under the optimal strategy. This phenomena does not depend on the specific numbers used in this example. Thus we may expect that voting for less than half the candidates, and in some cases voting for only one candidate (called *plunking* or *bullet-voting*), may be optimal.

Empirical evidence based on polling is in agreement with this expectation. Kellett and Mott (1977) asked respondents to choose from a list of candidates those whose nominations (for U.S. president) they felt they could support. For each of the Democratic and Republican parties, the respondents marked an average of about 35 percent of the eight candidates listed under each party. In response to an approval voting question on an exit poll following the 1981 New Jersey gubernatorial primaries (involving eleven Democratic candidates and eight Republican candidates), Brams, Urken, Sharrard, and Muzzio (1981) found that on the average 18 percent of the Democratic candidates and 25 percent of the Republican candidates were marked. On an approval voting question on a CPS survey preceding the 1980 U.S. presidential primaries, Brams and Sharrard (1979) found that those respondents who were willing to vote for any candidates at all selected an average of 39 percent of five candidates (three Democrats and two Republicans).

The first actual use of approval voting in a political setting occurred in 1983, when the Pennsylvania State Democratic Committee conducted a straw vote or preference poll for the eight announced Democratic presidential candidates (see section 8.4 for further details on the outcome). Of the 201 delegates who cast straw ballots, 58 percent voted for more than one candidate. Almost all of those who bullet-voted (plunked) for a single candidate voted for either Walter Mondale or John Glenn, the two front-runners at the time of the vote. Overall, the mean number of candidates voted for was 2.0, i.e., 25 percent of the eight candidates.

Thus the empirical evidence suggests that voters are likely to vote for less than 50 percent of the candidates under approval voting. As the number of candidates increases, the percent voted for under approval voting appears to decrease. When there is a large field of candidates, it may be expected that several will be unknown to many if not most voters. This was no doubt the case in the 1981 New Jersey gubernatorial primaries, where some of the twenty-one candidates may have "run for a lark."

Thus, for many voters, most of the candidates may have been rated below the weighted average for all candidates, with a large number of candidates with both low utility and low probability of winning lumped at the bottom. Thus, as we have seen, an optimal strategy may indeed involve far less than 50 percent of the candidates.

Formula (7.1), derived in section 5.5, defines a strategy with no skips. We also saw there that a more general version of (7.1), namely the criterion defined in chapter 5, note 3, could lead to a skipping strategy, but that such a situation would be rare. In any event, as we can see from Brams and Fishburn (1983, corollary 2.1), no admissible strategies for approval voting involve decapitation; i.e., it is never optimal to omit one's favorite.

7.3. STRATEGIC VOTING IN TWO-STAGE PROCEDURES BASED ON APPROVAL BALLOTING

Two-stage procedures occur when an initial ballot that narrows the alternatives or determines subsequent decision makers is followed by a second stage that may involve a different group of electors. Such two-stage rules include runoff elections, nomination procedures (in which a panel submits a list of individuals or alternatives from which a decision maker makes a final choice), and convention methods (in which the first stage selects delegates entitled to make the choice in the second stage). I consider here three explicit types of two-stage decision rules studied by Merrill and Nagel (1987).

(a) *Fixed slate-size rules* (FS). Out of the K original candidates, the S candidates who receive the most votes advance to the second stage (the value of S, $1 < S < K$, is fixed in advance). For example, a search committee may select S candidates from a larger pool, from which a single choice is made by an executive. An approval ballot followed by a runoff is a form of this rule in which $S = 2$.

(b) *Ballot-threshold rules* (BT). A candidate advances to the second stage if she attains a threshold T_b of ballots cast in the first stage.

(c) *Vote-threshold rules* (VT). A candidate advances to the second stage if she attains a threshold (proportion) T_v of the votes (not ballots) cast in the first stage.

Note that the distinction between BT and VT rules is peculiar to approval balloting; unless abstentions are recorded, the rules are equivalent under single-vote balloting. To analyze these two-stage rules, I assume, as in sections 5.4 and 5.5, a utility maximizing focal voter who assigns utilities u_1, ..., u_K to the candidates.

For the FS rule with slate of size S, I vary the definition of t_j slightly, now denoting by t_j the relative likelihood that candidate c_j will tie for Sth place, given that there is a tie, because this is the critical point for survival on the slate. This value is assumed to be estimated by the voter on the basis of polling or other information. Assume that every candidate who gets onto the slate has an equal chance of winning at the second stage. Given that there is a tie for Sth place (in which the tied candidates are unknown), the expected utility to the voter of a tied candidate is

$$\sum_{j=1}^{K} t_j u_j.$$

Hence, under FS, the voter has an incentive to cast a tie-breaking vote in favor of candidate c_i if

$$u_i > \sum_{j=1}^{K} t_j u_j. \tag{7.2}$$

In order to compare this condition with a comparable criterion for the BT and VT rules, let q_j be the voter's estimate of the relative likelihood that candidate c will attain or exceed threshold T_b. Here the expected mean utility of the slate that survives to the second stage is

$$\sum_{j=1}^{K} q_j u_j.$$

Again, assuming there is no information about the outcome in the second stage, this quantity is the expected utility to the focal voter of the slate. Voting for (or against) a candidate may permit the voter to add (or delete) that candidate to (or from) the slate, but not to replace a candidate, as under the FS rule. Thus, under BT rules, the voter has an incentive to cast an approval vote for candidate c_i if she is preferred to the expected utility of the slate, i.e., if

$$u_i > \sum_{j=1}^{K} q_j u_j. \tag{7.3}$$

Comparison of strategies for FS and BT rules thus reduces to an analysis of the probabilities t_j and q_j. Recall that $S > 1$; otherwise the second stage serves no purpose. Because the Sth position in the vote totals is an intermediate one, it seems reasonable that t_j will be highest for candidates of intermediate strength—in other words, the front-runner or a sure loser is less likely to be in a tie for the Sth place. Therefore, a plot of t_j versus proportion of the vote should look like figure 7.1.

Accordingly, in the FS case, $\Sigma\, t_j u_j$ will tend to be close in value to the utilities of candidates near the Sth position, since this average gives heavier weight to those utilities. But the trailing candidates near the Sth position have low utilities for most voters (that is why they are trailing). So $\Sigma\, t_j u_j$ tends to be low for most voters, and more so as S increases relative to K. Combined with (7.2), this conclusion leads to two results:

FS 1. *Under fixed slate-size rules, most voters have an incentive to cast approval votes for a relatively large proportion of candidates.*

FS 2. *This effect will be more pronounced when the slate is large relative to the number of candidates.*

In contrast, under BT rules, the likelihood of attaining the threshold will increase monotonically as candidate strength increases, yielding a plot like figure 7.2. This characteristic of q_j implies that the expected mean utility of the slate will be more strongly affected by the utilities of the front-runners, which are high for most voters, especially if T_b is high. Therefore, criterion (7.3) leads to these two results:

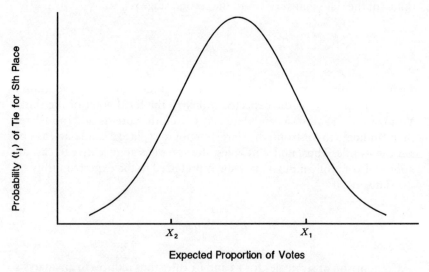

FIGURE 7.1. Plot of the Probability t_j that Candidate c_j Will Tie for Sth Place versus Proportion of the Vote
SOURCE: S. Merrill and J. Nagel, "The Effect of Approval Balloting on Strategic Voting under Alternative Decision Rules," *American Political Science Review* 81 (1987): 516; Figure 2, adapted with permission.

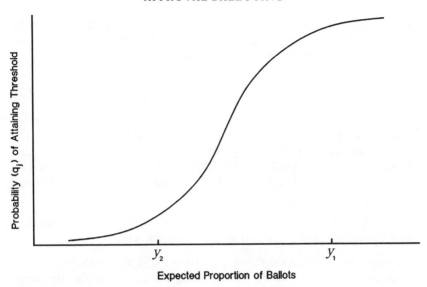

FIGURE 7.2. Plot of the Probability q_j that Candidate c_j Will Attain the Threshold T_b versus Proportion of the Ballots.
SOURCE: S. Merrill and J. Nagel, "The Effect of Approval Balloting on Strategic Voting under Alternative Decision Rules," *American Political Science Review* 81 (1987): 517; Figure 3, adapted with permission.

BT 1. *Under ballot-threshold rules, most voters have an incentive to cast relatively few approval votes.*

BT 2. *The tendency to truncate voting strategies will be stronger the higher the threshold.*

To investigate strategy under VT rules, assume that at most one candidate is near enough to T_v so that her prospects of attaining it can be affected by the focal voter. Let c_k denote this candidate near T_v and suppose that the focal voter wishes to know whether to vote for candidate c_i. If $i = k$, then criterion (7.3) applies: vote for c_i if $u_i > \Sigma\, q_j u_j$. Because this is the same as for BT rules, we obtain two similar results:

VT 1. *Under vote-threshold rules, most voters have an incentive to cast relatively few approval votes.*

VT 2. *The tendency to truncate voting strategies will be stronger the higher the threshold.*

However, if $i \neq k$, a vote for c_i has the potential of dropping c_k from the slate, because every additional vote increases the denominator on which

T_v is calculated and so dilutes the vote proportions of all other candidates—including c_k who is near the threshold. The voter should cast this sort of indirectly negative vote if

$$u_k < \sum_{j=1}^{K} q_j u_j. \qquad (7.4)$$

Criterion (7.4) is true for most voters, since the average $\Sigma\, q_j u_j$ of all candidates who attain the slate is typically higher than the utility u_k of a candidate who only marginally makes the slate. Hence it may be rational to vote for c_i, even though (7.3) fails. Thus, criterion (7.4) leads to the following result:

VT 3. *Under vote-threshold rules, most voters have an incentive to cast more approval votes than under ballot-threshold rules.*

The incentive to dilute the vote proportions under VT rules can generate either expansive or skipping strategies. As a corollary to the argument above, note that VT, unlike BT, is sensitive to the number of candidates. Under VT, a front-runner might encourage additional candidacies in order to pull rivals below T_v.

Computer simulations conducted by Merrill and Nagel (1987) substantiate the preceding analytic results. The proportion of candidates voted for under approval plurality drops from about 44 percent before a poll to from 36 to 39 percent after the poll, depending on its assumed effect on voter strategies. Under fixed slate-size rules, the tendency to truncate drops, as expected, as the size of the slate increases. For a ballot-threshold rule, the threshold, if high, is a greater inducement to plunk than an FS rule. Complete simulation results are given in Appendix D, table D.1.

7.4. The Effect of Collusion on Approval Voting

I now consider the effect of a coalition of voters with common utility profiles large enough to alter significantly, by an agreement on how to vote, the likelihood that candidates make the slate. Such action will be termed *collusion*. Under FS, a decision by the coalition to withhold votes has the potential to remove a candidate from the slate. Such an agreement would typically move the candidate's proportion of the vote from, say, position x_1 in figure 7.1 to position x_2, i.e., from better than Sth place to worse than Sth place. Because the graph is unimodal, the value of t_j is unlikely to change greatly, and in turn, criterion (7.2) will probably be little affected.

In contrast, under BT rules, the coalition's withholding of votes from candidate c_i may reduce her expected proportion of the ballots from y_1 to

y_2 (see figure 7.2), greatly decreasing the value of q_i. Hence, the weighted average $\Sigma\, q_j u_j$ of the utilities of candidates remaining on the slate rises, providing a further incentive toward truncation. This reverse snowball effect implies that it may be rational for a coalition to vote against a candidate who initially satisfies criterion (7.3) but who will fail to meet that condition after the coalition has withheld votes from some other candidate. We thus have additional results about the effects of collusion under the FS and BT rules:

FS 3. *Under* FS *rules, collusion creates only a modest inducement for a coalition to truncate or plunk.*

BT 3. *Under* BT *rules, collusion creates a strong inducement for a coalition to truncate and, often, to plunk.*

Simulations (see Appendix D, table D.2) indicate that collusion increases substantially the incentive for the coalition to plunk under approval plurality (from 15 to 40 percent for a 20 percent coalition). But the effect is dramatically stronger with a majority ballot threshold, where the incentive for the coalition to plunk increases to 64 percent.

7.5. Conclusions

Merrill and Nagel conclude that the negative skew of voter utilities and polling knowledge act in concert to encourage the restriction of approval ballots from the vote-for-half standard, and in many cases, to induce plunking. Although this effect occurs for single-stage approval voting (approval plurality), it is most pronounced in the presence of a threshold used in the first stage of a two-stage procedure. Collusion adds more fuel to the fire, especially in the threshold case.

Restriction of an approval ballot due to the negative skew of utilities is, in the sense of Merrill and Nagel, nonstrategic. Truncation induced by polling knowledge is strategic, but, in their terms, involves only a weak form of insincerity.

Under no decision rule for approval balloting is decapitation—failure to vote for one's first choice—a desirable strategy. This property of approval voting stands in sharp contrast to the frequent strategic desertion of one's favorite under single-vote plurality voting.

Among two-stage decision rules for approval balloting, the fixed slate-size rule is less conducive to ballot truncation than are threshold rules. Between threshold rules, a vote-threshold rule is less likely to induce truncation than a ballot-threshold rule. If a ballot threshold is used, a low threshold tends to reduce the otherwise high tendency toward truncation.

Weak insincerity, in the form of skipping a candidate to vote for one less preferred, may occur under either a fixed slate-size or a vote-threshold rule. Such a strategy, which involves the setting up of a pushover opponent for one's favorite, appears to be very risky and depends on accurate knowledge of how others will vote. For these reasons, it would seem unlikely that the pushover strategy would be commonly used in mass electorates.

Evaluation of the tendency of many decision rules for approval balloting to induce truncation or plunking should be tempered by quantitative estimates of the frequency for which such strategies might be optimal. Although the occurrence of optimal truncation is significant in nearly all simulation scenarios, the results suggest that in most cases well over half of the voters can optimally take advantage of the unique options of approval voting and cast a ballot for more than one candidate.

8

. . . .

EMPIRICAL ESTIMATES FOR
SINGLE-VOTE PLURALITY AND
APPROVAL VOTING

8.1. Introduction

Two of the major claims put forward by advocates of approval voting are that it tends to select the strongest candidate and that it reduces the incentives for infighting between candidates. Insofar as these arguments are valid, each is particularly pertinent to primary elections within a party.

In a primary election it is desirable to nominate a candidate with broad support who can serve as a viable standard bearer in the general election. Candidates who share the same constituency within a party can share support rather than fight each other for it, thus averting internal party rancor (see Kellett and Mott 1977). At the same time, vote totals for lesser candidates may more nearly represent their true support rather than only the residue left after desertions to front-runners (see Brams and Fishburn 1983).

If the "strongest candidate" is interpreted as the Condorcet candidate, the analyses in chapters 2, 4, and 6 of this book suggest that, under a wide range of assumptions, approval voting is significantly more likely to choose such a candidate than single-vote plurality voting. Approval voting, furthermore, can be expected to select the Condorcet candidate at least as often as any of the other procedures studied—provided that voters react strategically to aggregate information about how others may vote. If, however, they vote in ignorance, several voting systems, notably the Coombs, Borda, and Condorcet completion methods, and in some cases the Hare and runoff procedures, generally outperform approval voting with respect to Condorcet efficiency.

This chapter attempts to obtain empirical evidence to evaluate these claims on behalf of approval voting. The study reported in section 8.2 draws inferences about how voters might have voted under approval balloting in a three-way general election—the U.S. presidential race of 1968. Section 8.3 contains the results of a poll taken during the 1980 U.S. presidential primaries in which an explicit question was asked concerning the acceptability of candidates. Section 8.4 deals with a straw vote based on an approval ballot held among a group of party leaders just before the 1984 presidential primaries.

8.2. THE 1968 U.S. PRESIDENTIAL RACE

Using the CPS data for the 1968 U.S. presidential election in which George Wallace challenged the two major party nominees, Richard Nixon and Hubert Humphrey, Kiewiet (1979) assessed the likely effect of using approval voting. Under single-vote plurality, he found significant defections but few abstentions from those Wallace supporters who admitted that he had little chance of winning. As Kiewiet points out, Wallace's potential as a "kingmaker" in an electoral college deadlock and the desire by his supporters to "send a message" probably mitigated an even more serious erosion of support. Use of the thermometer scores suggests that Nixon was the Condorcet winner, beating Humphrey by about 7 percentage points, in contrast to the less than one-percent margin in the actual three-way popular-vote contest conducted under single-vote plurality rules.

Using the thermometer cut-point of 50 when possible, Kiewiet developed a set of plausible rules for determining whether a voter would vote for one or two candidates under approval balloting. Under these assumptions, he found that Wallace supporters would have cast more than twice as many approval votes for Nixon than for Humphrey.

As indicated in table 8.1, Kiewiet found a widening of the margin between the two major party nominees (to 9 percentage points), and an increase in the Wallace vote (from 14 to 21 percentage points), which almost exactly reversed his decline in the polls during the month immediately preceding the election.[1] Kiewiet also considered revised rules in which Nixon and Humphrey supporters strategically truncated their ballots if that proved necessary to avoid a vote for the other major party candidate (see table 8.1). Although the Nixon and Humphrey totals were reduced, Nixon would still have won by 6 percentage points.

These results suggest that the Condorcet candidate, Nixon, would almost certainly have won under approval voting. Kiewiet observes that the search for broad support (or acceptability) might augment existing centripetal pressures, leading to even greater ambiguity in campaign rhetoric.

---

[1] Due to multiple voting, the percent of ballots received by the candidates do not, of course, sum to 100.

TABLE 8.1. Estimates of Approval Balloting in the 1968 U.S.
Presidential Election

	Reported vote (%)	Estimated approval vote (%)	
		Sincere	Strategic
Richard Nixon	44	70	53
Hubert Humphrey	42	61	47
George Wallace	14	21	21

SOURCE: D. R. Kiewiet, "Approval Voting: The Case of the 1968 Presidential Election,"
Polity 12 (1979): 176, Table III; and 179, Table V; adapted with permission.

TABLE 8.2. Estimates for Single-Vote and Approval Balloting in 1980
New Hampshire Republican Primary

	Single-vote plurality (%)	Approval voting (%)
Ronald Reagan	50	58
George Bush	23	39
Howard Baker	13	41

Yet, at the same time, extremist or single-issue candidates might be encouraged by the opportunity to receive their true support without strategic erosion, while major candidates could remain relatively confident that minor parties would not be able to win the election.

8.3. THE 1980 REPUBLICAN PRESIDENTIAL PRIMARY IN NEW HAMPSHIRE

Although at this writing approval voting has been tested in the political arena only once (see section 7.2 above and section 8.4 below), approval voting questions have been asked as part of exit-poll questionnaires. ABC News, in an exit poll following the 1980 New Hampshire presidential primary, asked voters to indicate all the candidates whom they considered acceptable if they could have cast more than one vote. Table 8.2, based on the responses to this poll, indicates that the results of the Republican contest might have been significantly different had approval voting been in use.

In particular, Howard Baker, although he came in a weak third with only 13 percent of the vote under single-vote plurality, received 41 percent approval in the exit poll, coming in second, ahead of George Bush. As it was, Baker withdrew from the presidential race after a similar poor single-vote plurality showing in Massachusetts the following week. Had his residual support been reflected in the vote, he might well have remained in serious contention for much longer.

8.4. Overcoming a Catch-22:
The Use of Approval Voting among
Pennsylvania Democratic Leaders

Until 1983, as Jack Nagel has pointed out (1984), proponents of approval voting faced a Catch-22: they met resistance to testing the procedure in the political arena on the grounds that it was an untested procedure. Approval balloting has been used in a variety of private elections conducted in about twenty universities, the U.S. National Academy of Sciences, the Econometric Society,[2] and the Mathematical Association of America, and is employed in a modified form to select the secretary general of the United Nations. Its use in public elections, however, has been slow in coming.

This dilemma was finally broken in part when the Pennsylvania Democratic party under the leadership of State Chair Edward Mezvinsky used approval voting in a nonbinding presidential preference poll among Democratic party leaders at a meeting near Harrisburg on December 17, 1983. The precarious process by which academics and political decision-makers interacted to bring about this first public test of approval voting is described by Nagel (1984).

The field of candidates, for whom 201 Pennsylvania Democratic leaders cast approval ballots, consisted of the eight Democratic contenders for the 1984 Democratic presidential nomination. The fact that all eight were accepted as serious candidates (although Walter Mondale and John Glenn were given the best chances of winning at that time), provided a better-than-usual test of the expectation that most voters would approve of more than one candidate.

Despite predictions of plunking (bullet-voting) by a number of politicians, 58 percent of the voters voted for more than one candidate. As in-

[2] The Econometric Society uses a modification of approval voting in which a voter may cast two votes for one candidate and one vote for each of as many others as he wishes. Such a procedure is actually a hybrid, equivalent to adding the vote totals of approval voting and single-vote plurality.

dicated in section 7.2, the average number of candidates voted for was 2.0, or 25 percent of the candidates on the ballot. Nearly all plunks were for one or the other of the two front-runners, votes that may well have been optimal. Multiple voting in the Pennsylvania preference poll is reported in table 8.3, along with the number of distinctions between candidates for each number of votes.

Note that a voter makes the most distinctions—and hence has the most potential opportunities to be decisive—if he votes for half (in this case four) of the candidates. The number of distinctions made by the voter, however, drops off only slightly as the voter deviates from the vote-for-half strategy. Voting for between two and six of the eight candidates makes at least 75 percent of the possible distinctions.

However, as we saw in chapter 7, some distinctions are more likely to be important to the voter than others. For example, distinctions between two front-runners or between a front-runner and a trailer are generally more important than one between trailers. Since front-runners are more likely to be near the top of most voters' preference orders, distinctions made between them tend to be more valuable to most voters, establishing an incentive to vote for less than half of the candidates.

The results of the Pennsylvania poll are given in table 8.4. Two candidates demonstrate majority or near-majority support, while four others show substantial support in the 15–20 percent range. Most supporters of

TABLE 8.3. Multiple Voting in the Pennsylvania Presidential Preference Poll

Number of voters	Votes cast per voter	Number of candidates not voted for	Number of distinctions
1	0	8	0
84	1	7	7
73	2	6	12
19	3	5	15
14	4	4	16
6	5	3	15
2	6	2	12
1	7	1	7
1	8	0	0

CHAPTER 8

TABLE 8.4. Approval Voting Results of Pennsylvania
Presidential Preference Poll

Candidate	Approval vote (%)
Walter Mondale	74
John Glenn	45
Ernest Hollings	20
Jesse Jackson	16
Alan Cranston	15
Gary Hart	14
George McGovern	6
Reuben Askew	5

Jesse Jackson also voted for front-runner Walter Mondale—an option not available to them under the usual single-vote plurality system.

Knowledge of approval ballots permits us to analyze shared support between candidates and thus to identify subsystems or affinity groups of candidates who share the same constituency. Such information is of interest to candidates as they map out their campaign strategies, although it would be pertinent to their decisions whether an approval ballot was to be used in the official election or just as an information poll.

A measure of shared support between candidates c_i and c_j, introduced by De Maio, Muzzio, and Sharrard (1985), can be defined as the ratio $(A_{ij} - E_{ij})/E_{ij}$, where A_{ij} is the actual number of shared voters, and E_{ij} is the expected number of shared voters. Computation of the latter assumes that candidate c_i shares the same percentage of candidates c_j's votes as candidate c_i shares with all other candidates.

Analysis of the Pennsylvania State Democratic Committee poll highlights two affinity groups. One consists of Jackson, Hart, McGovern, and Cranston; the other involves Hollings, Glenn, and Askew. In addition there is a connection between Jackson and Mondale. This structure reflects the conventional classification into liberals and conservative Democrats in that race.

Study of the ABC approval voting exit poll for New Hampshire in the 1984 Democratic primary gives a similar picture. This time, however, Hart occupies a link between the two groups, with Mondale more closely associated with Hart than Jackson, perhaps because of there being fewer black voters in New Hampshire than in Pennsylvania.

8.5. Conclusions

Analysis of voter preferences in the 1968 U.S. presidential election (section 8.2) and in the Democratic primaries preceding that election (section 6.5) suggest that approval voting would more likely have chosen the Condorcet candidate (or at least augmented his victory) than single-vote plurality. The latter data also suggest that approval voting totals would have correlated more strongly than those of single-vote plurality with social utility.

Under approval voting, support for George Wallace in 1968 and Howard Baker and Jesse Jackson in 1980 would likely have more nearly matched their true support than showed under single-vote plurality. This helps substantiate the claim that under approval voting there is less desertion of favorites in favor of front-runners. There is also less need for candidates with a shared constituency to rely on negative campaigning against each other.

9

. . . .

OTHER CRITERIA FOR

ASSESSING VOTING SYSTEMS

9.1. Introduction

This chapter evaluates the seven voting procedures introduced in chapter 1 for each of the criteria embodied in Arrow's axioms. Furthermore, several systems are shown to have the property of minimality, i.e., they offer, with trivial exceptions, no strategies that cannot be optimal for any voter.

Section 9.2 discusses Arrow's conditions, with emphasis on the criteria of monotonicity and independence of irrelevant alternatives. In section 9.3, I demonstrate that the three plurality voting systems are all minimal and, in fact, two of them—single-vote plurality and approval voting—permit exactly the residual strategies left when nonoptimal strategies are discarded from two other systems—cumulative voting and cardinal-measure voting, respectively. Section 9.4 deals with a modification of cardinal-measure voting, which not only is minimal but under which, for certain circumstances, the optimal strategies are direct reflections of the voter's utilities.

9.2. Assessment of Multicandidate Voting Systems using Arrow's Axioms

I assess the tendency of the voting systems under study to satisfy the four conditions in Arrow's impossibility theorem (see section 1.5): monotonicity, independence of irrelevant alternatives, nonimposition, and nondictatorship. All seven systems satisfy nonimposition and nondictatorship. It is simple to check that single-vote plurality, approval voting, and the Borda count are monotone, and the same is true for any Condorcet completion method which, like Black's prescription, uses a monotone contingency method.[1]

---

[1] To see that any Condorcet completion method is monotone if the contingency method is

All elimination methods, however, including the Hare, Coombs, and runoff systems, violate monotonicity, i.e., a voter may harm a candidate by placing her higher in her preference order (while all other relative preferences remain unchanged) or help a candidate by lowering her in her preference order. Basically, this paradox can occur because altering preferences changes the order in which candidates are eliminated. Raising one's preference for a focal candidate above that of a pushover may permit a third candidate to remain in contention long enough to eliminate the focal candidate, as the following example, in which C is the pushover, illustrates.

Initial preferences

3 voters	2 voters	6 voters	4 voters	2 voters
A	A	B	C	C
B	C	C	A	B
C	B	A	B	A

If the last two voters, each having preference order CBA, raise their preference for B, so that their preference order is then BCA, a win by B in either Hare or runoff is, as indicted below, converted to a win by A, the last choice of both of these voters.

	Voting with initial preferences			*Voting with altered preferences*		
	A	B	C	A	B	C
First ballot	5	6	6	5	8	4
Second ballot	—	9	8	9	8	—
		B wins			*A wins*	

The strategic implications for elimination methods resulting from the violation of monotonicity are discussed in section 6.6. Such manipulation not only requires a sophisticated strategist, but, in the light of empirical evidence, appears to be feasible less often than other forms of insincere voting that plague the Borda, Coombs, and single-vote plurality systems.

Arrow's axiom concerning independence of irrelevant alternatives prescribes that the entry of a new candidate (or the withdrawal of a current candidate) should not alter the social ranking of the remaining candidates,

---

monotone, let A be the winner under the system for some voter profile. If there is a Condorcet candidate, it is A, and will continue to be if some voter moves A up in her ranking. If there is no Condorcet candidate, A is the contingency winner. If a voter moves A up, only A could thereby become a Condorcet candidate. Otherwise, A remains the contingency winner because the contingency rule is monotone. Hence A wins with the altered preferences. The remainder of the social preference ordering may, however, not be preserved when the focal voter's altered ballot creates a Condorcet candidate where there was none before.

provided relative rankings of the other candidates by individuals remain unchanged. Entry of a new candidate does not alter the majority ordering of the original candidates, if one exists, and in particular, it cannot upset a Condorcet candidate unless a majority prefer the new candidate to the original Condorcet candidate.

Although all of the seven voting systems violate in some circumstances the criterion of independence of irrelevant alternatives, there is significant variation in the extent of this violation, as indicated by the simulation results in table 9.1.[2] More infringements of the criterion occur for single-vote plurality (19 percent of elections), runoff (10 percent), and approval voting (9 percent) than for the other systems. Numerous violations can be expected for single-vote plurality because of the opportunity for a new entry to squeeze a previous winner, permitting a candidate located on the opposite spatial side to win.

Approval voting performs less well as the number of candidates decreases, or if the negative-of-distance utility is used, breaching the criterion more often than single-vote plurality for some simulation scenarios. In general, however, the effect of new entries on vote totals is more wrenching for the single-vote plurality system than for other plurality systems like approval voting and the Borda count. The latter two often produce close contests that are more easily overturned by an additional candidacy than the frequently one-sided contests that obtain under single-vote plurality, where the vote totals can be changed sharply without altering the winner.

TABLE 9.1. Violations of Independence of Irrelevant Alternatives

Voting system	Violations (%)	Mean correlation before/after
Single-vote plurality	19	0.85
Runoff	10	n.a.
Hare	6	n.a.
Approval voting	9	0.98
Borda	7	0.99
Coombs	1	n.a.
Black	0.1	n.a.

n.a.: not applicable.

[2] The simulation involved 1,000 elections and a spatial model with two dimensions, correlation = 0.5, relative dispersion = 1.0, and the Shepsle utility function.

To some extent, these close races under Borda and approval voting are an artifact of the simulation assumption that all voting decisions are based on spatial positions. In real elections, some candidates can be expected to have nonspatially-based advantages (involving, e.g., popularity, experience, or financial resources). A measure that is independent of nonspatial factors may be more indicative of the effect of new entries in real elections. For this reason, the correlations between the vote totals of the residual candidates before and after the new entry are presented for plurality systems in table 9.1. Correlation measures the degree of the violations that occur. The Borda and approval voting totals are much less affected, according to this measure, by a new entry than is single-vote plurality. This conclusion is corroborated by the empirical evidence from the 1972 Democratic presidential primaries reported above in section 6.5.

9.3. Minimal Voting Systems

Often two or more voting systems may appear to permit quite different strategies, but the set of (potentially) optimal strategies of one may include that of the other as a proper subset, that is, the first may be reducible to the second. Once this is recognized, it would seem best, *ceteris paribus*, to choose the one that is the simplest to understand and implement.

For a given voting system with K candidates, a permissible strategy is termed *potentially uniquely optimal* (PUO) if there are voter utilities u_i and subjective probabilities t_{ij} such that expected utility is strictly optimized for this strategy (see section 5.4). Following Weber (1977), we will say that a voting system is *minimal* if all its permissible strategies (abstentions excepted) are PUO strategies.

I will first describe heuristically some results for minimal voting systems. In particular, single-vote plurality is a minimal system. Cumulative voting is not, but it is reducible to single-vote plurality. That is to say, single-vote plurality voting permits precisely those options of cumulative voting that are PUO strategies and no others, suggesting that single-vote plurality is clearly superior to cumulative voting for single-winner races, since the latter adds nothing but additional, but never optimal, strategies with which to confuse the voter. I say "confuse the voter" because such strategies, although never rational, might well be used by voters through ignorance.

Recall that under cumulative voting the voter is assigned M votes that she may apportion to the candidates at will. This voting principle is indeed used in multivacancy elections, such as the selection by stockholders of a corporate board of directors and (until 1982) the election of the Illinois House of Representatives (see Blair 1973 for further discussion). For single-winner races, however, under the criterion of expected utility, it is always in the interest of the voter to transfer any of her M votes that she might have placed on a less attractive candidate to a more attractive one, where attractiveness should be measured in terms of the strategic value $S(c_i)$ introduced in section 5.4. Thus the voter's optimal strategy under cumulative voting is to cast all her votes for the candidate with the highest value of $S(c_i)$. But this is also her optimal strategy under single-vote plurality voting.

This fact can be illustrated by the following simple example. Suppose in a three-candidate race, a voter prefers A over B and B over C. Supplied with a total of, say, 10 votes to apportion among these candidates, let us say that she initially decides to cast 6, 3, and 1 votes to A, B, and C, respectively. Since the voter, however, prefers A to C, she will clearly gain in expected utility (provided equiprobable outcomes are assumed) by transferring the one vote for C to A. Likewise, expected utility will increase if the three votes for B are transferred to A as well. Hence, the optimal strategy is to cast all ten votes for A.

By a similar argument we can see that approval voting (abstentions excepted) consists precisely of the optimal strategies of a system in which each voter can rate the candidates on a common scale and casts votes equal in number to her ratings, i.e., the cardinal-measure system. To maximize expected utilities, only the extremes of the scale should be used, i.e., the voter should dichotomize the candidates, just as in approval voting. Like single-vote plurality and approval voting, the Borda system can be shown to be minimal in the same sense (see Merrill 1981).

These results all follow from a characterization of the PUO strategies as *extreme points*[3] of the set of permissible strategies satisfying a certain property. The theorems are stated and proved—along with their corollaries for specific voting systems—in Appendix E.

Note that PUO strategies are always admissible strategies in the sense of Brams and Fishburn (1978), provided that the latter concept is modified to take account of cardinal rather than ordinal ratings. Admissible strategies, however, need not be potentially uniquely optimal. The difference between the two concepts is that an admissible strategy is undominated for the set of all contingencies (contingencies are specified in terms of the t_{ij} in the present model), whereas a PUO strategy is undominated for a specific contingency. Since a voter can be expected to have partial but imperfect knowledge of the contingency in a particular election, it would appear

[3] A point is called an *extreme point* of a convex set if it is not interior to any line segment contained in the set.

that both concepts shed light on the voter's strategic decision. The results of this section are summarized in the following statements:

CONCLUSION 1. *Cumulative voting (in a single-winner election) is reducible to single-vote plurality in the sense that the two systems have equivalent optimal strategies. In the same sense, cardinal-measure voting is reducible to approval voting.*

CONCLUSION 2. *With the exception of abstentions (and, equivalently, voting for all candidates under approval voting), single-vote plurality, approval voting, and the Borda count are all minimal voting systems.*

9.4. THE STANDARD-SCORE VOTING SYSTEM

The characterization in the preceding section of potentially uniquely optimal strategies as a set of extreme points suggests that we might be able to construct a minimal voting system by specifying as permissible set a region of Euclidean space R^K, all of whose points are extreme. In fact, a sphere is such a set, and the subset of it defined in Appendix F specifies a permissible region consisting entirely of extreme points that are potentially uniquely optimal.[4] Furthermore, the voting system defined by this permissible region is a simple modification of the cardinal-measure voting system, but one in which the system does not induce the voter to strategically avoid all but the extremes of the scale.

This voting system—although its invention was motivated by the foregoing considerations—can be described much more simply. The procedure, to be called the *standard-score voting system*, is defined as follows:

RULE 1. *The balloting method is identical to that for cardinal-measure voting: rate each candidate on a fixed scale, say, 0 to 100.*

RULE 2. *The decision rule is different: for each voter separately, replace her ratings r_i by their statistical standard scores, i.e.,*

$$Z_i = (r_i - \mu)/\sigma, \tag{9.1}$$

where μ and σ are the mean and standard deviation of the voter's ratings. For each candidate, sum the standard scores over all voters. The candidate with the largest total wins.

Recall that for each voter, her set of standard scores has mean zero and standard deviation 1. Thus, the standard scores are independent of the

---

.[4] The hollow sphere is not convex, but that is not a necessary condition for a voting system to be minimal.

scale and position used by the voter (the use of a fixed interval such as 0 to 100 is only a convenience).

As was shown in section 5.4, under cardinal-measure voting, the optimal strategy for a utility maximizer is to dichotomize the candidates using the extremes of the scale as ratings. By contrast, under standard-score voting, the voter is rewarded for reporting ratings intermediate between her extremes, since they reduce the standard deviation in the denominator of the standard score. The standard scores of such a voter are expanded relative to those of a voter using only the extremes of the scale, enhancing her effect on the outcome. The expected utilities in table 9.2, computed for equiprobable outcomes from formula (5.2)[5], illustrate these effects.

For the voter with utilities for the four candidates given in table 9.2, the optimal strategy (100, 100, 0, 0) under cardinal-measure voting yields a higher expected utility (4,000) than does the vote (100, 70, 50, 0), which exactly reflects her utilities. The latter gives an expected utility of 3,533. By contrast, under standard-score voting, the straightforward strategy (100, 70, 50, 0) yields an expected utility of 97.1, higher than the 80 offered by the strategy (100, 100, 0, 0).[6] If outcome probabilities are not equally likely (i.e., if the t_{ij} are not all the same), the optimal strategies still employ the full scale but may not be exactly in proportion to utilities.

TABLE 9.2. Example of Voter Profile for Cardinal-Measure and Standard-Score Voting

Candidate	Utility	Z_i	Cardinal-measure		Standard-score voting	
			Strategy 1	Strategy 2	Strategy 1	Strategy 2
A	100	1.24	100	100	100	100
B	70	0.41	70	100	70	100
C	50	−0.14	50	0	50	0
D	0	−1.51	0	0	0	0
Expected utility			3,533	4,000	97.1	80.0

[5] For equiprobable outcomes with four candidates, $t_{ij} = 1/3$ for $i \neq j$. Note that comparison of expected utilities across voting systems is meaningless.

[6] In particular, in a decision under uncertainty, standard-score voting is a preference revealing procedure that avoids the compensatory weighting of votes needed when, say, the Clarke tax method (see Straffin 1980, section 3.5) is applied to voters with nonhomogeneous resources.

Coleman (1982) derives a procedure equivalent to the standard-score system. He solves directly the problem of choosing a transformation of votes-as-cast into votes-as-counted so that the voter will maximize expected utility by casting votes that are a linear transformation of her utilities. If Z_i denotes the standard score as defined by (9.1), the Coleman value for votes-as-counted is $(Z_i + \mu/\sigma)/\sqrt{6}$, i.e., a linear transformation of the standard-score value. The standard-score system, because of the complexity of its decision rule, should be recommended only for a mathematically knowledgeable electorate.

9.5. Conclusions.

We have seen that cumulative voting is reducible to single-vote plurality, and cardinal-measure voting is reducible to approval voting. Both of these reduced methods together with the Borda count are minimal in the sense that all permissible voting strategies are potentially uniquely optimal.

The characterization of optimal strategies provides other dividends, including the construction of the standard-score system. A modification of cardinal-measure voting, this procedure specifies that the votes-as-counted are the statistical standard scores of the votes-as-cast. Unlike cardinal-measure voting, standard-score voting does not reduce to approval voting, but rather it offers optimal intermediate strategies that closely reflect the voters' utilities.

Violation of the monotonicity criterion is perhaps the most disturbing flaw in the elimination voting systems, including the Hare, runoff, and Coombs procedures, although this fault appears difficult to detect or exploit in practice in mass elections. All of the voting systems we have studied are sensitive to some extent to the entry of new candidates, but the effect is more pronounced for single-vote plurality and, in certain situations, for approval voting. Such a sensitivity opens the way for a faction to manipulate the outcome by introducing a candidate not intended to win but to draw support away from a rival.

10

. . . .

CONCLUSIONS

The concept of majoritarian rule seems clear in principle; to implement it when there are three or more candidates is not. The logical difficulties of specifying a winner—first observed two centuries ago by Condorcet—are still with us and, in light of Arrow's theorem, will not go away. Still, the exigencies of practical social choice demand that winners be chosen from multicandidate elections. From the richness of electoral procedures that have been proposed, one must choose schemes suited to specific needs, evaluating each in turn against appropriate criteria.

We have considered the choice of the Condorcet candidate as the most natural extension of the majoritarian principle to single-winner, multicandidate elections. An alternative criterion—that the candidate with the greatest average intensity of support should be chosen—is measured by social utility. Accordingly, Condorcet efficiency—the tendency that a voting system will choose the Condorcet candidate, if one exists—and social-utility efficiency, which measures the social or average utility of the winner, permit us to assess voting systems from two points of view. Although the candidate with the highest social utility is frequently not the Condorcet candidate, comparative analysis of voting systems according to the two measures of efficiency shows remarkably similar results.

Evaluation of voting systems in this book by computer simulation has rested on two general types of models of voting behavior: random-society and spatial models. Aside from differences in detail, the two types of models yield generally comparable results. Under the constraint of sincere voting, one remarkable conclusion concerning Condorcet and social-utility efficiency shines through the myriad of varying assumptions: the consistent weak showing of the single-vote plurality system. This procedure has by either measure the lowest efficiency of all procedures under study for almost all scenarios.

Under a spatial model, furthermore, those systems that place a premium on first-place votes, including single-vote plurality, Hare, and runoff, permit centrist candidates to be squeezed by more extreme candidates. This effect, which greatly decreases both measures of efficiency for tightly clustered candidates, is however partially dampened by the perceptual uncertainty of voters of the candidates' positions.

In most voting situations, voters have some knowledge of how others may vote. Strategies that employ this information affect balloting behavior differentially for different voting systems. The Hare system appears to be the most resistant to practical strategic behavior. A sophisticated voter may, however, exploit the non-monotonicity of the procedure by awarding a first preference to a pushover in the hope of derailing a chief rival of his favorite.

Under approval voting, optimal strategies follow the relatively straightforward rule: vote for candidates whose utilities exceed the mean. Deviations from this rule usually take the form of truncation or less commonly expansion, but only rarely involve skipping down the preference order. Single-vote plurality encourages voters to desert expected losers. Borda, Coombs, and all Condorcet completion methods encourage a voter to punish his favorite's chief rival with a last-place vote. The runoff system occupies an intermediate position between the single-vote plurality and the Hare scheme. Under runoff, there is some tendency to desert expected losers, and the pushover strategy is easier to implement than under Hare because a voter may alter his vote between ballots.

Strategic voting likewise exerts a differential impact on the tendency for a voting procedure to choose the Condorcet candidate or a candidate with high intensity of support. The Condorcet and social-utility efficiencies of the Hare and runoff systems, partly because of their resistance to practical strategic voting, are little affected by the possibility of manipulation. Manipulation of the Borda, Coombs, and Condorcet completion methods, all of which permit the punishment of nonpreferred but leading candidates while still giving first preferences to one's favorite, tends to reduce the chances that the Condorcet candidate wins.

By contrast, the Condorcet and social-utility efficiencies of single-vote plurality and approval voting tend to increase under strategic voting, since optimal strategies in each system focus the voters' attention on the front-runners without offering incentives to punish them. In cases where manipulation is unlikely (as may be the case in an evaluation panel charged with selecting an award winner) the Borda count, Coombs, or a Condorcet completion method might be appropriate. If, however, strategic voting is to be expected, the approval voting, Hare, and runoff procedures are less vulnerable to subversion and to the resulting loss in Condorcet and social-utility efficiency.

In choosing a single winner to hold executive office, an electoral outcome signifying a broad mandate may be desirable, both in primaries to choose party nominees and in general elections. Such an objective may often be achieved by a candidate representing a centrist position within the electorate. In a large electorate following a symmetric spatial distribution, the Condorcet candidate is closest to the center of the distribution. Condorcet efficiency is, accordingly, an indication of the tendency for the voting system to choose centrists as winners. The low Condorcet efficiency of the single-vote plurality method and the conclusions of Cox (1987) that this procedure fails to have a multicandidate equilibrium at the voter median indicate that unlike the multivote procedures, single-vote plurality need not induce winning-oriented candidates to seek the ideological center of the electorate.

Insofar as gross manipulation is perceived as a threat to the legitimacy of the outcome, methods that are relatively resistant to manipulation, such as Hare, approval voting, and runoff are desirable. Approval voting does permit an additional level of strategic behavior, which, although it is unlikely to call into question the legitimacy of the outcome, adds a complicating dimension to the voter's decision making. Designating an approved set of candidates, however, places fewer demands on the voter than a complete preference order, and in contrast to runoff, approval voting requires only one ballot.

Single-vote plurality, despite is flaws, not only is a model of simplicity, but appears to act as a brake on factionalism and as an incentive for voters to focus on the leading contenders. Accordingly, single-vote plurality in a polity that is neither decentralized nor dominated by a single centrist party may act as an inducement toward a two-party system, and if successful, it may obviate the need for multicandidate procedures. On the other hand, multivote systems such as approval voting, Hare, and runoff would appear particularly well suited for primary elections within a political party, where a strong standard bearer is sought who can represent a unified party.

One objective of this book has been to establish the relevance of mathematical models in this evaluative process. This has been valuable, even though in many cases it is not possible to prove categorical results for the voting systems under investigation. Rather, the theorems are hedged with conditions or the inferences are based on simulations and are statistical in nature.

Yet the many instances of corroborating results—the similar effects of random-society and spatial models, the rough agreement in ranking of voting systems by Condorcet and social-utility efficiency under a variety of assumptions, the repeated vulnerability of Hare, runoff, and single-vote plurality to the squeeze effect in different settings—all add confirming notes to the inferences. Empirical data from polls and elections, limited as it is, tends to support the conclusions from theoretical arguments and simulation studies.

Choice by a voting system of the Condorcet candidate or a candidate with high average intensity of support is likely to enhance the legitimacy of the system in the eyes of the electorate. By these criteria, under sincere voting, single-vote plurality falls far behind the other procedures. The differential impact of strategic voting, however, on the two measures of efficiency suggests that the most dependable systems are approval voting, Hare, and runoff. Although strategic voting is inevitable for any reasonable voting system, knowledge of severe manipulation undermines the electorate's faith in the procedure. The potential for such insincere voting calls into question the use of the Borda, Coombs, and possibly even Condorcet completion methods for public elections.

Simplicity of a procedure—such as that of single-vote plurality or approval voting—helps voters understand and respect the outcome. Despite the acceptance of Hare in Australia, this method, like others that require that the voter submit a complete preference order, may encounter practical obstacles to implementation in other mass electorates.

Although single-vote plurality has been advocated for general elections as a disincentive to factionalism, its rating well below that of all other systems studied when measured by many other criteria suggests that alternative methods be tested. For primary elections, in which fragmentation is a less salient issue, approval voting would have in addition to the advantage of simplicity the virtues of relatively high Condorcet and social-utility efficiencies and relative freedom from the more perverse aspects of insincere voting. Although these virtues are partially shared by the runoff and Hare systems, the latter two procedures have lower social-utility efficiencies, violate monotonicity, are less robust to variations in assumptions about voter behavior, and runoff lacks the simplicity and elegance of a single ballot.

Ultimately, the selection of a voting system depends on the size and composition of the electorate and the political objectives for which elections are held. This study and the methodology on which it is based are intended to facilitate that choice.

APPENDIX A

A STATISTICAL MODEL FOR

CONDORCET EFFICIENCY

Appendix A incorporates the simulation results from chapter 2 on Condorcet efficiency under spatial model assumptions into a statistical model. This model will be embodied in an equation (with statistical error term) that is intended to explain or predict a dependent variable in terms of several independent variables.

Using Condorcet efficiency as the dependent variable, the model predicts efficiency from the following independent variables: (1) the number of candidates, (2) the dimension and correlation structure of the spatial model, and (3) the relative dispersion of candidates to voters. The model is in the form of logistic multiple regression with calibration data from 35,000 simulated elections.

The coefficients of the model equation quantitatively assess the relative effects of the independent variables on Condorcet efficiency. The statistical model also predicts the response (Condorcet efficiency) for values of the independent parameters not directly available from the simulation results. That is, the model allows one to predict Condorcet efficiency for input parameters not tested in an actual simulation. Since the possible combinations of parameters (particularly those regarding correlation structure and relative dispersion) are immense, it is impossible to simulate all cases.

To develop a statistical model for Condorcet efficiency, Merrill (1985) ran thirty-five simulated scenarios, each involving one thousand elections. As in the simulations reported in chapter 2, each election involved a fresh electorate of 201 voters generated from a multivariate normal distribution. For each scenario, two hundred sets of candidates were generated from a multivariate normal distribution, each set of candidates being associated with five of the one thousand electorates.

Each simulated scenario involves a particular setting of parameters: the number of candidates (from three to seven), the number of spatial dimensions (from one to four), the correlation structure, and the relative dispersion of candidates to voters. Two correlation structures were used in estimating regression coefficients: one in which all off-diagonal correlations are 0.0 and one in which all off-diagonal correlations are 0.5. The relative dispersion (RD) of candidates to voters varies from 0.5 to 1.414 ($= \sqrt{2}$), although most runs use 0.5 and 1.0.

Since Condorcet efficiency is a proportion (or a percent), that cannot be expected to be normally distributed over a wide range of values, a logistic multiple regression (with weights proportional to $p(1 - p)$, where p is the Condorcet efficiency) is appropriate (see Neter and Wasserman 1974, 329–35). Under logistic regression, the dependent variable, p, is replaced by

$$y = \log[p/(1 - p)], \tag{A.1}$$

which is more nearly normally distributed. The logistic transformation defined by (A.1) is similar to that used in probit analysis.

Preliminary analysis suggested that the logistic dependent variable varies approximately linearly with respect to the logarithm of the number of candidates, the logarithm of the number of dimensions, and the logarithm of relative dispersion over the range 0.5 to $\sqrt{2}$. (As relative dispersion decreases below 0.5, Condorcet efficiency continues to drop, but at a reduced rate.)

Incorporating dimension and correlation structure into a single parameter streamlines the model. To this end, one seeks a parameter that agrees with dimension for uncorrelated variates. If some variates are degenerate, the parameter should equal the number of nondegenerate variates, that is, the number of nonzero entries in the diagonalized form of the correlation matrix. We can achieve this result by defining the *generalized dimension* (*GD*) of a multivariate normal spatial model as

$$GD = d^2 / \Sigma \, \lambda_i^2, \tag{A.2}$$

where d is the ordinary dimension, and $\{\lambda_i\}$ are the eigenvalues of the correlation matrix (see the Glossary for the definition of eigenvalue).

To justify (A.2), notes that if the variates are uncorrelated (but nondegenerate), each $\lambda_i = 1$ and $GD = d$. If m of the variates are uncorrelated and the rest degenerate, then m of the eigenvalues are equal to d/m, and the others are equal to 0. It follows that

$$GD = d^2 \, / \sum_{i=1}^{m} d^2/m^2 = d^2/(d^2/m) = m.$$

Intuitively, this property is desirable, since as the correlation between two variates approaches unity (that is, as one of them approaches degeneracy), we wish GD to decrease by one unit.

For example, for a two-dimensional spatial model with correlation r between the issues, $GD = 2/(1 + r^2)$. Thus, if there is no correlation ($r = 0$), $GD = 2.0$. If $r = 1$, $GD = 1.0$, reflecting the fact that complete correlation between the two issues is tantamount to a one-dimensional model. If the correlation between voter position on the two issues is 0.5, then $GD = 1.6$, representing a degree of diversity in voter opinion intermediate between one salient issue and two uncorrelated issues. Since, for more than two dimensions, the correlation matrix involves several parameters (there are $d(d - 1)/2$ parameters, where d is the number of dimensions), incorporation of correlation structure and number of dimensions into a single parameter constitutes a substantial reduction in the parameters of the model.

The resulting statistical model is:

$$\log[p/(1 - p)] = b_0 + b_1 \log (K - 2) + b_2 \log (GD) + b_3 \log (RD) + \epsilon, \quad \text{(A.3)}$$

where, for conveniences of interpretation, all logarithms are to base 2. If the number K of candidates is two, Condorcet efficiency is unity (for any voting system and independently of the other variables). Accordingly, log $(K - 2)$ is used in place of $\log(K)$. Table A.1 presents regression statistics for each voting system.

The first purpose of a statistical model is as an explanatory device. The

TABLE A.1. Logistic Regression Statistics for Condorcet Efficiency Using Model (A.3)

System	b_0	b_1	b_2	b_3	R^2	Mean absolute deviation
Single-vote plurality	1.51	−1.11	0.93	2.06	0.95	0.027
Runoff	2.95	−1.30	1.38	2.78	0.96	0.025
Hare	2.67	−1.22	1.58	2.63	0.96	0.026
Approval	1.84	−0.65	0.85	(0.15)	0.87	0.021
Borda	3.06	−0.51	0.60	0.39	0.83	0.013
Coombs	5.92	−1.17	0.44	1.39	0.85	0.015

SOURCE: S. Merrill, "A Statistical Model for Condorcet Efficiency based on Simulation under Spatial Model Assumptions," *Public Choice* 47 (1985): 392, Table 1; reprinted with permission.
NOTE: All coefficients except for the one in parentheses are significant at the 0.05 level.

regression coefficients in table A.1 reveal the relative effect of variation of parameters on Condorcet efficiency. For all systems, Condorcet efficiency drops as the number of candidates increases—as the negative signs for the coefficient b_1 indicate—but it drops significantly less (at the 0.05 level) for approval voting and the Borda system. It increases as either GD or RD increase for all systems (as the positive signs for b_2 and b_3 indicate), with the increases significantly greater (0.05 level) for the runoff, Hare, and (for RD) single-vote plurality systems.

Section 2.3 presents a detailed discussion of the squeeze effect that tends to reduce Condorcet efficiency if the relative dispersion (RD) of candidates is low. This effect is particularly strong for the single-vote plurality, runoff, and Hare systems, for which the garnering of first-place votes in a large field is essential to winning. One may conjecture that the increase of Condorcet efficiency as the generalized dimension (GD) increases is a reflection of the same phenomenon. Increasing the number of spatial dimensions appears to provide more "elbow room" for voters and candidates, lessening the tendency of the Condorcet candidate (usually the most centrally located candidate) to be squeezed by her opponents.

Table A.2 provides an assessment of the predictive capacity of the model by comparing model values for Condorcet efficiency with values obtained directly from simulation scenarios not used in model calibration. Scenario no. 1 is that used by Chamberlin and Cohen (1978) for medium dispersion; for scenario no. 2, the parameters (eigenvalues) are chosen by a random process.

Comparison of model estimates and direct simulation values for p (Condorcet efficiency) is also assessed in the last column of table A.1, which gives the mean of the absolute deviations between these two quantities. The accurate predictive power of the model supports our contention that, for purposes of explaining Condorcet efficiency, we can collapse spatial dimension and correlation structure into a single parameter.

The model appears to fit well over the range of the number of candidates and spatial dimensions studied, although less well for the one-dimensional case. It is not adequate for RD below 0.5, however, or for the Coombs system in a one-dimensional model. Condorcet efficiency for the latter scenario approaches unity as the number of voters increases. It appears that Condorcet efficiency for the Coombs system may suffer a discontinuity as GD approaches 1.

To summarize, the purpose of this appendix is to organize a collection of simulation results—assessing the tendency under spatial model assumptions of certain multicandidate electoral systems to choose Condorcet candidates—into a statistical model that is both explanatory and pre-

TABLE A.2. Model and Simulated Condorcet Efficiencies for Several Spatial
Model Scenarios Not Used in Model Calibration
Values (for Voting Systems) in Percentages

Scenario No.:	1		2		3		4	
K:	4		4		4		5	
GD:	1.95		2.90		1.49		1.00	
Eigenvalues:	(2.72, 0.82, 0.30, 0.16)		(1.57, 1.48, 0.93, 0.02)		(3.25, 0.25, 0.25, 0.25)		(1.00)	
RD:	1.00		1.00		1.00		0.50	
Condorcet efficiency	Model	Simulation	Model	Simulation	Model	Simulation	Model	Simulation
Single-vote plurality	71	68	78	77	55	46	17	16
Runoff	89	89	93	92	76	74	21	23
Hare	89	89	94	94	76	73	21	25
Approval	80	80	85	86	71	73	61	59
Borda	90	91	92	93	86	90	78	78
Coombs	97	97	98	98	95	96	86	100

SOURCE: S. Merrill, "A Statistical Model for Condorcet Efficiency Based on Simulation under Spatial Model Assumptions," *Public Choice* 47 (1985): 394, Table 2; reprinted with permission.

dictive. Assessment of the model suggests that, for most cases of interest, a logistic multiple linear regression with three independent variables is sufficient to model the relation of Condorcet efficiency to number of candidates, number of spatial dimensions, correlation structure, and relative dispersion of candidates and voters.

APPENDIX B

JUSTIFICATION OF

THE SHEPSLE UTILITY FUNCTION

Assume that candidates and voters are drawn from a bivariate normal spatial model with correlation $= 0$. The Shepsle utility function (Shepsle 1972), defined by

$$u(d) = \exp(-d^2/2)$$

has the following theoretical justification. If the voter is at the center of the spatial model, the distance d from voter to candidate has a Weibull distribution with shape parameter 2 and scale parameter 0.5, i.e., d has distribution function

$$F(d) = 1 - \exp(-d^2/2)$$

(see Johnson and Kotz 1970). If we wish to obtain a utility function $u(d)$ uniformly distributed on $[0,1]$, we need only define $u(d) = F(d)$, or more simply

$$u(d) = 1 - F(d) = \exp(-d^2/2),$$

which is except for a constant the normal density function—the form suggested by Shepsle.

If the voter is not at the center, computer calculation indicates that d has a distribution that is approximately Weibull with distribution function

$$F(d) = 1 - \exp(-d^2/b)$$

where $b > 2$. For voters at the median distance ($d = 1.18$) from the center, b is approximately 4.

Using psychophysical evaluation of candidates by respondents, Snider (1979) found that the utilities of the voters he studied followed approximately the distribution function $G(u) = \sqrt{u}$. If we wish utilities to follow this distribution function, we set

$$u(d) = G^{-1}[\exp(-d^2/b)] = \exp(-2d^2/b),$$

where G^{-1} denotes the inverse of G. For $b = 4$, this becomes

$$u(d) = \exp(-d^2/2),$$

which is exactly the normal density. Thus for a voter at approximately median distance from the center, the set of voter utilities generated from the normal-density (Shepsle) utility function should follow approximately a square root distribution, i.e., a plot of utility versus candidate rank (high ranks used for the more preferred candidates) will have the shape of the curve $u = (\text{rank}/M)^2$ where M is the number of candidates (see figure B.1). This follows since the expected value of rank/M is a discrete approximation of $G(u)$, so this plot is simply the inverse of the distribution function $G(u) = \sqrt{u}$.

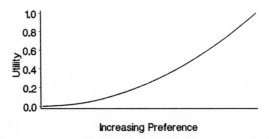

FIGURE B.1. Plot of Voter Utility versus Preference for the Shepsle Utility Function.
SOURCE: S. Merrill and J. Nagel, "The Effect of Approval Balloting on Strategic Voting under Alternative Decision Rules," *American Political Science Review* 81 (1987): 512; Figure 1, adapted with permission.

On the other hand, if a negative-of-distance utility (i.e., $u(d) = -d$) is used, the distribution function of voter utilities is given by

$$G(u) = \exp(-u^2/2), \quad u < 0,$$

so that a plot of utility versus candidate rank will look like that in figure B.2.

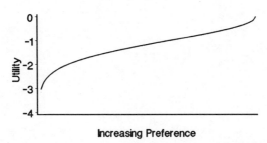

FIGURE B.2. Plot of Voter Utility versus Preference for the Negative-of-Distance Utility Function.

The sharp distinction this latter curve makes between low-ranked candidates seems questionable for most voters, who are likely to lump several little-known candidates near the bottom of their utility scales. It may, however, constitute a reasonable model for a voter who primarily wishes to vote against one or two abhorred candidates.

I would argue that a crucial criterion in selecting a utility function is the nature of the distribution of preferences it implies, a distribution that can be empirically tested. The greater plausibility and empirical support for a distribution like that in figure B.1 suggest that the Shepsle utility function may be more realistic than the apparently simpler utility function defined in terms of the negative of distance.

APPENDIX C

PROOFS OF THEOREMS

5.1 AND 5.2

Appendix C presents proofs of theorem 5.1, which specifies optimal strategies using the Savage regret criterion when voting under uncertainty, and theorem 5.2, which states a simple form for the expected utility function $U(V)$.

THEOREM 5.1. In a K-candidate race, the optimal strategies under the criterion of Savage regret are:

(a) Single-vote plurality: Vote for one's first choice.
(b) Borda: Assign votes in order of preference.
(c) Approval: Vote for all candidates c_i for whom
$$u_i > (u_1 + u_K)/2.$$

PROOF. Recall that the voter exercises power only if her vote $V = (v_1, \ldots, v_K)$ is decisive for some pair of candidates c_i and c_j in the sense that a reversal of v_i and v_j would alter the winner. (It is assumed that a tie for first place after the focal voter has voted is resolved by lot.) The payoff when the focal vote casts vote V and is decisive for candidates c_i and c_j with $i < j$ is given by

$$(v_i - v_j)(u_i - u_j).$$

Note that $(v_i - v_j)$ is proportional to the probability that the focal voter will be decisive, while $(u_i - u_j)$ represents her payoff if she is decisive. The term $(v_i - v_j)$ is included because the potential for reversing the result is proportional to the quantity $(v_i - v_j)$ regardless of the relative strengths of the candidates or the voter's knowledge of their strengths. This follows because the number of voters is assumed to be large so that the probability that, say, c_j leads c_i by exactly m votes before the focal voter votes is approximately the same for each possible value of m, where m is small.

We assume, without loss of generality, that

$$1 = u_1 \geqslant u_2 \geqslant \ldots \geqslant u_K = 0,$$

117

and that $0 \leq v_i \leq M$, for a positive constant M determined by the voting system. Thus the best that the focal voter can attain when she is decisive for c_i and c_j is $M(u_i - u_j)$, so the regret for vote V is given by

$$R(V; c_i c_j) = [M - (v_i - v_j)] (u_i - u_j).$$

Thus the maximal regret for vote V is given by

$$MR(V) = \max_{i < j} [M - (v_i - v_j)] (u_i - u_j). \tag{C.1}$$

We derive the optimal regret strategy for each voting system separately.

Under single-vote plurality, $M = 1$. If the voter votes for her first preference, i.e., for c_1,

$$MR(V) = \max_{1 < i < j} [1 - 0] (u_i - u_j) = u_2.$$

Intuitively, her greatest regret is failure to distinguish between c_2 and c_K when they are tied. If, on the other hand, the voter votes for a candidate other than c_1,

$$MR(V) \geq [1 - (v_1 - v_K)](u_1 - u_K) > (u_1 - u_K) = 1.$$

Thus voting for c_1 (the voter's first preference) yields the least maximum regret and is the optimal Savage regret strategy. (If $u_i = 1$ for several candidates, voting for any of them is an optimal strategy.)

Under approval voting, we may assume, without loss of generality, that $v_1 = 1$ and $v_K = 0$, since any vote V not satisfying these conditions is dominated by a vote for which they are true. We show that the strategy represented by the vote $V^* = (v_1^*, \ldots, v_K^*)$, defined by setting

and
$$\begin{array}{llll} v_i^* = 1 & \text{if} & u_i > 0.5 \\ v_i^* = 0 & \text{if} & u_i \leq 0.5, \end{array}$$

is an optimal Savage regret strategy.

Since $v_i \leq 1$ for any approval voting strategy V, $M = 1$, and by (C.1)

$$MR(V) = \max_{i < j} [1 - (v_i - v_j)](u_i - u_j).$$

It is not hard to check that

$$MR(V^*) = \max_{v_i^* = v_j^*} (u_i - u_j) \leq 0.5.$$

If, on the other hand, $V \neq V^*$, there exist k such that either ($v_k = 0$ and $u_k > 0.5$) or ($v_k = 1$ and $u_k \leq 0.5$). In the first case,

$$MR(V) \geq [1 - (v_k - v_K)](u_k - u_K) = u_k > 0.5,$$

and in the second case,

$$MR(V) \geq [1 - (v_1 - v_k)](u_1 - u_k) = 1 - u_k \geq 0.5.$$

It follows that $MR(V^*) \leq 0.5 \leq MR(V)$, so that V^* is an optimal Savage regret strategy.

We now show that the optimal Savage regret strategy for the Borda count is $V^* = (K - 1, K - 2, \ldots, 1, 0)$. Noting that here the constant m is $K - 1$, we have

$$MR(V^*) = \max_{i < j} \{M - [(K - i) - (K - j)]\}(u_i - u_j)$$
$$= \max_{i < j} [M - (j - i)](u_i - u_j).$$

Again it suffices to show that

$$[M - (j - i)](u_i - u_j) \leq MR(V)$$

for all $i < j$ and for any vote V permissible under the Borda count. Let us fix i and j such that $i < j$. First note that

$$(u_i - u_j) \leq (u_m - u_n) \tag{C.2}$$

for all $m = 1, \ldots, i$, and $n = j, \ldots, K$. In fact, we will show that

$$[M - (j - i)](u_i - u_j) \leq \max_{\substack{m \leq i \\ n \geq j}} [M - (v_m - v_n)](u_m - u_n) \leq MR(V).$$

The second inequality follows from the definition (C.1) since the maximum in (C.3) is taken over a subset of the pairs (m,n) with $m < n$. If the first inequality in (C.3) is not the case, we see from (C.2) that for all $m \leq i$ and $n \geq j$,

$$M - (j - i) > M - (v_m - v_n),$$

or more simply,

$$(j - i) < (v_m - v_n). \tag{C.4}$$

But since the v_m and v_n must take distinct values from the set $\{K - 1, \ldots, 0\}$,

$$\min_{m \leq i} v_m \leq (K - i) \quad \text{and} \quad \max_{n \geq j} v_n \geq (K - j).$$

Hence

$$\min_{\substack{m \leq i \\ n \geq j}} (v_m - v_n) \leq (K - i) - (K - j) = (j - i).$$

But this contradicts (C.4), completing the proof of the theorem.

(Most of the proof of theorem 5.1 is taken from S. Merrill, "Strategic Voting in Multicandidate Elections under Uncertainty and under Risk," in *Power, Voting, and Voting Power*, ed. M. Holler, 182–84. Copyright by Physica-Verlag; reprinted with permission.)

THEOREM 5.2. If $V = (v_1, \ldots, v_K)$ is any permissible strategy for the focal voter and a specified voting system, and U is the expected utility function given by (5.1), then

$$U(V) = \sum_{i=1}^{K} S(c_i)v_i. \tag{C.5}$$

PROOF. First observe that

$$2U(V) = \sum_{i=1}^{K} \sum_{j=1}^{K} (u_i - u_j)(v_i - v_j)t_{ij}$$

$$= \sum_{i=1}^{K} \sum_{j=1}^{K} (u_i - u_j)v_i t_{ij} - \sum_{i=1}^{K} \sum_{j=1}^{K} (u_i - u_j)v_j t_{ij}.$$

By interchanging i and j, we may write

$$- \sum_{i=1}^{K} \sum_{j=1}^{K} (u_i - u_j)v_j t_{ij} = - \sum_{j=1}^{K} \sum_{i=1}^{K} (u_j - u_i)v_i t_{ji}$$

$$= + \sum_{i=1}^{K} \sum_{j=1}^{K} (u_i - u_j)v_i t_{ij}.$$

Hence

$$2U(V) = 2 \sum_{i=1}^{K} \sum_{j=1}^{K} (u_i - u_j)v_i t_{ij} = 2 \sum_{i=1}^{K} S(c_i)\, v_i.$$

APPENDIX D

SIMULATION RESULTS FOR

APPROVAL BALLOTING WITH

ALTERNATIVE DECISION RULES

To substantiate the analytic results in sections 7.3 and 7.4, Merrill and Nagel (1987) conducted a number of computer simulations. Each basic run involved five hundred elections, each with five candidates and one hundred voters chosen from a standard bivariate normal spatial model (correlation = 0). Because of the arguments presented in Appendix B, the Shepsle utility function $u(d) = \exp(- d^2/2)$ was used. Candidates were ranked in descending order by a poll (i.e., candidate 1 is expected to finish first, etc.).

For approval plurality (AP), three different assumptions were used to assign values to the t_j:

(a) t_j proportional to the proportion p_j of the vote that c_j receives in a simulated election assuming pure sincerity;
(b) the Brams poll assumption;
(c) t_j proportional to $(5,4,3,2,1)$.

As indicated in table D.1, the truncation of ballots under AP is reflected strikingly in the increase in optimal plunking from 15 percent to about 24 percent under assumptions (a) and (c) and to 43 percent under the Brams rule.

To assess FS rules, assumptions of type (c) were used. Specifically, for $S = 2,3,$ and 4, the t_j were chosen proportional to $(3,4,3,2,1)$, $(1,2,3,2,1)$, and $(1,2,3,4,3)$, respectively. The results in table D.1 show, as expected, that the tendency to truncate drops as the size of the slate increases.

For the BT rule, the weights were taken proportional to values of a function of the form depicted in figure 7.2, with the slope at the threshold denoted c. A 50 percent ballot threshold drops the percentage of candidates voted for from 44 to 36 and raises the plunking percentage from 15 to 35,

TABLE D.1. Likelihood of Optimal Plunking under Approval Voting without Collusion: Simulation Results

Model	Number of Candidates	% of voters plunking		% of candidates voted for	
		Before poll	After poll	Before poll	After poll
Approval plurality ($S = 1$)[a]					
(a) $s_i = x_i$	5	15	24	44	39
(b) Brams's rule	5	15	43	44	36
(c) s_i proportional to (5,4,3,2,1)	5	15	23	43	39
Fixed slate-size rule[a]					
$S = 2$	5	15	21	43	40
$S = 3$	5	15	16	44	43
$S = 4$	5	14	12	44	47
Ballot threshold rule[a]					
$T_b = 0.5$ $(c = 2)$	5	15	35	44	36
$T_b = 0.2$ $(c = 2)$	5	15	20	44	41
Alternative utility functions ($S = 1$)[b]					
$u(d) = \exp(-d^2/1)$	5	31	40	37	34
$u(d) = \exp(-d^2/2)$	5	15	24	44	39
$u(d) = -d$	5	2	10	52	45
Variation of number of candidates ($S = 1$)[b]					
3 candidates	3	64	73	45	42
4 candidates	4	34	48	44	39
5 candidates	5	15	24	44	39
8 candidates	8	22	2	43	38

SOURCE: S. Merrill and J. Nagel, "The Effect of Approval Balloting on Strategic Voting under Alternative Decision Rules," *American Political Science Review* 81 (1987): 519, Table 1; adapted with permission.

[a] Each simulation is based on 500 elections, each involving 100 voters (standard errors for plunking percentage are about 1 percentage point).

[b] Each simulation is based on 100 elections, giving standard errors of 2 to 3 percentage points.

i.e., constitutes a greater inducement toward truncation than a fixed slate-size rule. A low ballot threshold, however, has a much reduced effect.

Table D.1 also presents simulation results for alternative utility functions. Although the plunking and truncation percentages are strongly affected in an absolute sense, the effects of polling appear to act uniformly over the various functions. By contrast, the percentage of candidates voted for is remarkably stable when the number of candidates in the race is varied from three to eight. One may speculate, however, that the negative skew of the utility distribution may increase with the number of candidates, which may explain the reduced percentage approved in large primaries, as reported from polling data in section 7.2.

The effects of collusion among coalitions representing 10 percent and 20 percent of the voters for approval plurality and for a majority BT rule were also simulated (see table D.2). Merrill and Nagel imagine the coalition operating in an ocean of voters voting in ignorance, while the coali-

TABLE D.2. Likelihood of Optimal Plunking in the Presence of a Colluding Coalition: Simulation Results

Model	Number of candidates	% of oceanic voters plunking		% of colluding coalitions plunking
		Before poll	After poll	
Fixed slate-size rule ($S = 1$)				
10% coalition	5	16	23	31
20% coalition	5	15	24	40
Ballot threshold ($T_b = 0.5; c = 2$)				
10% coalition	5	16	37	49
20% coalition	5	16	38	64

SOURCE: S. Merrill and J. Nagel, "The Effect of Approval Balloting on Strategic Voting under Alternative Decision Rules," *American Political Science Review* 81 (1987): 520, Table 2; adapted with permission.

NOTE: Each simulation based on 100 elections, each involving 100 voters. Standard errors for oceanic voters: 2 to 3 percentage points; for colluding coalitions: 4 percentage points.

tion uses the knowledge of their own collusion as the equivalent of polling data. The coalition is assumed to know only the distribution of candidate support within the ocean, not the identity of the candidates having that support. Each simulation run involves one hundred elections, each consisting of one hundred voters. Collusion greatly increases the coalition's incentive to plunk, especially in the presence of a high ballot threshold.

APPENDIX E

CHARACTERIZATION OF THE
POTENTIALLY UNIQUELY
OPTIMAL STRATEGIES AS EXTREME
POINTS OF THE PERMISSIBLE SET
OF STRATEGIES

A linear function $U : R^K \to R$ will be called an *expected utility function* if there exists real numbers u_i, $i = 1, \ldots, K$, and probabilities t_{ij}, $j = 1$, $\ldots, K$, such that $t_{ii} = 0$ and $t_{ji} = t_{ij}$, for which (5.1) holds. This definition is only a reinterpretation of our previous use of the term expected utility. In what follows, I will refer to a permissible strategy by the more technical term *feasible strategy*. For a given voting system with K candidates, a feasible strategy V^* is *potentially uniquely optimal* (PUO) if there exists an expected utility function $U : R^K \to R$, such that $U(V^*) > U(V)$, for any other feasible strategy V. To show that a point V^* in the feasible set S of strategies is extreme (see Glossary), it suffices to find a linear function $U : R^K \to R$, such that $U(V^*) > U(V)$ for all $V \in S$ other than V^*.

THEOREM E.1. If the feasible set S of a plurality voting system is convex, then the potentially uniquely optimal strategies are extreme points of S.

PROOF. If V^* is a PUO strategy, then there exists an expected utility function U such that $U(V^*) > U(V)$ for all $V \in S$ other than V^*. Thus V^* is extreme.

The direct converse of this theorem is not true. An abstention $V_0 = (0, \ldots, 0)$ is, trivially, an extreme point for any voting system not permitting negative votes, but it is not potentially uniquely optimal. (V_0 is optimal only if the voter is indifferent, but then all strategies are optimal.) To

125

obtain a less trivial example, consider the voting system for which $K = 2$ and $0 \leq v_i \leq 2$, $i = 1,2$, and $v_1 + v_2 \leq 3$. Then the strategies $(2,1)$ and $(1,2)$ are extreme points, but neither is a PUO strategy.

Before stating a partial converse of Theorem E.1, we need a lemma and some definitions. If U is an expected utility function, then $\Sigma\, S(c_i) = 0$. The following lemma states that this property characterizes expected utility functions.

LEMMA E.1. If $U : R^K \to R$ is a linear function defined by

$$U(V) = \sum_{i=1}^{K} a_i\, v_i,$$

then U is an expected utility function if

$$\sum_{i=1}^{K} a_i = 0.$$

PROOF: Fix t, $0 < t < 1$. Set $t_{ij} = t$ for all i, j, $i \neq j$, and $u_i = a_i/tK$. Then

$$S(c_i) = \sum_{j=1}^{K} (u_i - u_j)t_{ij} = tKu_i - t \sum_{j=1}^{K} u_j$$

$$= a_i - (1K) \sum_{j=1}^{K} a_j = a_i.$$

Hence

$$U(V) = \sum_{i=1}^{K} S(c_i)v_i,$$

so that by the proof of Theorem 5.2 (see Appendix C), U is an expected utility function.

DEFINITION E.1. A voting system with feasible set S is called *polyhedral* if there exists an integer m, a $K \times m$ matrix A, and an m-vector B such that $S = \{V \in R^K : VA \leq B\}$.

Let $V^* = (v_1^*, \ldots, v_K^*)$ be an extreme point of the set S of feasible strategies for a polyhedral voting system specified by the constraints $VA \leq B$. For each constraint $\Sigma\, a_{ij}v_i \leq b_j$, the intersection of S with the hyperplane $\{V : \Sigma\, a_{ij}v_i = b_j\}$ is called a *face* of S. Denote by F_j, $j = 1, \ldots, r$, the faces of S that contain V^*. In fact

$$V^* = \bigcap_{j=1}^{r} F_j.$$

Renumbering the constraints if necessary, the hyperplane containing each face F_j is orthogonal to the vector $A_j = (a_{1j}, \ldots, a_{Kj})$ of coefficients of the jth constraint. For all $V \in S$, and for each $j = 1, \ldots, r$,

$$\sum_{i=1}^{K} a_{ij} v_i \leq \sum_{i=1}^{K} a_{ij} v_i^*,$$

with equality holding only if $V \in F_j$.

DEFINITION E.2. Denote by C_V^* the open cone generated by $\{A_1, \ldots, A_r\}$, i.e., the set of vectors of the form

$$\sum_{j=1}^{r} b_j A_j,$$

where $0 < b_j$ for $j = 1, \ldots, r$.

THEOREM E.2. Let V^* be an extreme point of the set S of feasible strategies for a polyhedral voting system. Then V^* is a PUO strategy if there exists

$$A \in C_V^* \quad \text{with} \quad \sum_{i=1}^{K} a_i = 0. \tag{E.1}$$

PROOF. Suppose that (E.1) holds. Define $U : R^K \to R$ by

$$U(V) = \sum_{i=1}^{K} a_i v_i.$$

By Lemma E.1, U is an expected utility function. Since $A \in C_V^*$,

$$A = \sum_{j=1}^{r} b_j A_j,$$

where $0 < b_j$ for $j = 1, \ldots, r$. In particular,

$$a_i = \sum_{j=1}^{r} b_j a_{ij}. \tag{E.2}$$

Thus if $V \in S$, but $V \neq V^*$,

$$U(V) = \sum_{i=1}^{K} a_i V_i = \sum_{i=1}^{K} \sum_{j=1}^{r} b_j a_{ij} v_i$$

127

$$= \sum_{j=1}^{r} b_j \sum_{i=1}^{K} a_{ij}v_i < \sum_{j=1}^{r} b_j \sum_{i=1}^{K} a_{ij}v_i^* = U(V^*),$$

the inequality being strict, since V cannot lie in all faces $\mathbf{F}_j$, whereas all $b_j > 0$. It follows that V^* is potentially uniquely optimal. This completes the proof of Theorem E.2.

WE NOW apply these theorems to several specific voting systems. The cumulative voting system is polyhedral, defined by the constraints $VA \le B$, where $A = (a_{ij})$ is a $K \times (K+1)$ matrix given by $a_{ii} = -1, a_{i,K+1} = 1, i = 1, \ldots, K$, and $a_{ij} = 0$ otherwise, and $B = (b_j)$ is a $(K+1)$ −vector given by $b_j = 0, j = 1, \ldots, K, b_{K+1} = M$. Under cumulative voting the set of feasible strategies is a K-dimensional tetrahedron whose extreme points (vertices) lie at the origin and the points $(M,0, \ldots, 0)$, $(0,M,0, \ldots, 0), \ldots, (0, \ldots, 0,M)$. By Theorem E.1 only these strategies can be potentially uniquely optimal. In fact all extreme points, except the origin (abstention), are PUO strategies. To see this, it suffices to look at the strategy $(M,0, \ldots, 0)$. It is the intersection of K faces, determined by constraints $v_1 + \ldots + v_k \le M$ *and* $-v_i \le 0$, for $i = 2, \ldots, K$. These constraints determine constraint vectors $A_1, \ldots, A_K$, where $A_1 = (1, \ldots, 1)$ and $a_{ii} = -1, i = 2, \ldots, K$, and $a_{ij} = 0$ otherwise. Setting $b_1 = 1$ and $b_j = K/(K-1)$ and defining a_i by (E.2) shows that $(M,0, \ldots, 0)$ satisfies condition (E.1) of Theorem E.2.

If each feasible strategy under cumulative voting is multiplied by $1/M$, it is clear that the strategies that are potentially uniquely optimal under cumulative voting correspond to the full set of feasible strategies under single-vote plurality voting in a large electorate. This justifies the claim in section 9.3.

Cardinal-rating voting is also polyhedral, the feasible set being a K-dimensional cube. All coordinates of each extreme point (vertex) are either one or the other extreme (M_1 or M_2) of the scale available to the voter. Applying the transformation $v_i \to (v_i - M_1)/(M_2 - M_1)$, this set of extreme points corresponds to the full set of feasible strategies available under approval voting. In fact, all extreme points (except the two in which all components are equal) are PUO strategies. To see this, note that each extreme point is the intersection of K faces, with corresponding constraint vectors $A_1, \ldots, A_K$, where A_i is the coordinate vector e_i if $v_i = M_2$ and $A_i = -e_i$ if $v_i = M_1$. If n is the number of candidates receiving vote M_2, set $b_i = 1/n$ for those candidates and $b_i = 1/(K-n)$ for the remaining candidates. It follows again from condition (E.1) of Theorem E.2 that an extreme point is a PUO strategy unless $n = 0$ or $n = K$.

To relate the Borda system to Theorem E.2, consider the convex set

S consisting of the vectors $V = (v_1, \ldots, v_K)$ such that for all integers $k = 1, \ldots, K$ and for all subsets $v_{i_1}, \ldots, v_{i_k}$ consisting of exactly k of the $v_1, \ldots, v_K$, we have

$$- (K - k) \leq [v_{i_1} + \ldots + v_{i_k}]/k \leq (K - k),$$

where, for each candidate, v_i denotes the symmetric Borda score specifed by the number of candidates ranked lower, minus the number of candidates ranked higher. It can be shown (Merrill 1981, 133, note 4) that the feasible strategies permitted by the Borda system are precisely the extreme points of the polyhedral voting system with feasible set S.

To see that any extreme point V^* of S is a PUO strategy for S, assume without loss of generality that $v_i^* = K + 1 - 2i$, i.e., that the v_i^* are in decreasing order. Then V^* is the intersection of $2K$ faces determined by constraints

$$v_1 + \ldots + v_k \leq k(K - k),$$

and

$$-v_{K+1-k} - \ldots - v_K \leq (K - k)^2$$

for $k = 1, \ldots, K$. Setting $b_j = 1$ for $j = 1, \ldots, 2K$, we have $a_i = K + 1 - 2i$ (see E.2), so that in fact $a_i = v_i^*$ and $\Sigma a_i = 0$. Hence by Theorems E.1 and E.2, the set of extreme points of S (and hence the set of feasible Borda strategies) is precisely the set of PUO strategies of S.

APPENDIX F

DERIVATION OF

THE STANDARD-SCORE

VOTING SYSTEM

Suppose each voter is permitted to choose any real numbers $v_1, \ldots, v_K$ such that

$$\sum_{i=1}^{K} v_i = 0 \quad \text{and} \quad \sum_{i=1}^{K} v_i^2 = K.$$

Under this nonlinear set of constraints, the feasible region is the intersection of a hyperplane with a K-dimensional sphere and the quadratic programming problem of maximizing $U(V)$ can be solved by Lagrange multipliers. This method implies that there exists a constant λ such that $v_i = \lambda\, S(c_i)$ for all i, $i = 1, \ldots, K$. The constraint $\sum v_i^2 = K$ requires that

$$\lambda = \sqrt{K}\, S(c_i)/[\sum S(c_i)^2]^{1/2}.$$

It then follows from the argument used to prove Theorem E.2 that all feasible strategies are potentially uniquely optimal. In other words, the voter's optimal strategy is to assign votes to the candidates in proportion to the strategic values $S(c_i)$.

The following theorem indicates the form of the optimal strategy when the voter votes in ignorance.

THEOREM F.1. If all t_{ij} are the same, the optimal strategy consists of votes v_i, for which

$$v_i = (1/\sigma)[u_i - (1/K) \sum_{j=1}^{K} u_j],$$

where σ is the standard deviation of the $u_1, \ldots, u_K$.

PROOF. Note that

130

$$v_i^2 = K[\underset{j}{\textstyle\sum}(u_i - u_j)]^2/\underset{i}{\textstyle\sum}[\underset{j}{\textstyle\sum}(u_i - u_j)]^2$$

$$= K^3[u_i - (1/K)\underset{j}{\textstyle\sum}u_j]^2/\{K^3\underset{i}{\textstyle\sum}[u_i - (1/K)\underset{j}{\textstyle\sum}u_j]^2/K\}$$

so that

$$v_i = [u_i = (1/K)\underset{j}{\textstyle\sum}u_j]/\sigma.$$

Thus, in the case of voting under uncertainty with equiprobable out-comes, the optimal votes-as-counted v_i are simply the statistical standard scores of the values $u_1, \ldots, u_K$ and the optimal strategy of the voter represents a sincere reflection (i.e., a positive linear transformation) of his cardinal ratings.

GLOSSARY

Admissible strategy. A feasible voting strategy is admissible if there is no other feasible strategy that is preferred to it for at least one contingency and at least as good as it in all other contingencies.

Approval voting system. The approval voting system consists of a balloting method that permits the voter to give one vote to each of any number of candidates and the plurality decision rule, i.e., the candidate with the most votes wins.

Black voting system. The Black system is a Condorcet completion method that involves a ballot that requires a full preference order. The decision rule selects the Condorcet candidate, if one exists; if not, the Borda rule is used.

Borda voting system. The Borda system (or Borda count) specifies that the voter submit a full preference order; the decision rule assigns scores to each preference, usually $K - 1, K - 2, \ldots, 0$, respectively, to the preferences in descending order. The candidate with the highest total score wins.

Bullet-voting. See Plunking.

City-block metric. In a spatial model the city-block metric measures distance along the vertical and horizontal lines of a grid, i.e., the distance between points $x = (x_i, \ldots, x_n)$ and $y = (y_1, \ldots, y_n)$ is given by the quantity $\Sigma |x_i - y_i|$.

Collusion. Collusion is any effort by a coalition of voters to alter, by agreement on how to vote, the outcome of an election.

Condorcet candidate. The Condorcet candidate in a multicandidate election is that candidate, if one exists, who could beat each of the others in separate pairwise contests, i.e., is preferred to each of the others by a majority.

Condorcet completion method. A Condorcet completion method is a voting system that chooses the Condorcet candidate, if one exists, and specifies a contingency rule if one does not.

Condorcet efficiency. The Condorcet efficiency of a voting procedure is the proportion or percentage of a class of elections (for which a Condorcet candidate exists) in which the voting system chooses the Condorcet candidate as winner.

Convex set. A convex set in an N-dimensional space is a set such that for

133

any two points in the set, the line segment connecting them is completely in the set.

Coombs voting system. The Coombs voting system requires a full preference order. The decision rule provides that the candidate with the most last-place votes be eliminated, and that the next-to-last-place votes for this candidate be transferred to augment the last-place totals of the remaining candidates. This process is repeated until only one candidate remains and is declared the winner.

Copeland voting system. The Copeland system is a Condorcet completion method, which requires a full preference order. The decision rule chooses the Condorcet candidate, if one exists; if not, the candidate who could beat the most others in pairwise contests is chosen. If two or more candidates tie for winning the most two-way contests, the result is indeterminate.

Correlation. The correlation between two random variables is a statistical measure of the tendency of the two variables to vary in concert.

Correlation matrix. The correlation matrix of n random variables is an $n \times n$ table of the pairwise correlations of the variables.

Density. The probability density function of a random variable is a function whose integral over any interval represents the probability that the variable assume a value in this interval.

Decision under risk. A decision under risk is a choice of strategy when the probabilities of possible outcomes are known.

Decision under uncertainty. A decision under uncertainty involves a choice of strategy when the probabilities of possible outcomes are unknown.

Dimension of a spatial model. The dimension of spatial model denotes the number of coordinates designated in each point in the space. Each such coordinate may be intended to represent the position of a participant (voter or candidate) on a specific issue or characteristic.

Distribution function. A probability distribution function of a random variable is the cumulative version of the probability density function, i.e., the distribution function, evaluated at a value x, is the probability that the variable will be less than or equal to x.

Dodgson voting system. The Dodgson voting system is a Condorcet completion method, requiring a full preference order. The system chooses the Condorcet candidate, if one exists; if not, that candidate is chosen whose maximum loss to others in pairwise contests is least.

Dual culture. A dual culture is an electorate in which all or most voters have one of two preference orders, usually opposite in nature, or alternatively, an electorate following a bimodal distribution in a spatial model.

134

Eigenvalue. An eigenvalue of a square matrix A is a number λ such that there exists a nonzero vector x with $Ax = \lambda x$, i.e., multiplication by A preserves direction.

Euclidean distance. The Euclidean distance between two points $x = (x_1, \ldots, x_n)$ and $y = (y_1, \ldots, y_n)$ is given by the square root of the expression $(x_1 - y_1)^2 + \ldots + (x_n - y_n)^2$.

Expected utility. Expected utility is the average utility weighted by the probabilities of possible outcomes, i.e., give n possible outcomes with probabilities $p_1, \ldots, p_n$, and utilities $u_1, \ldots, u_n$, respectively, the expected utility is $\Sigma\, p_i u_i$.

Extreme point of a convex set. A point is called an extreme point of a convex set if it is not interior to any line segment contained in the set.

Focal voter. A focal voter is a voter, intended to represent a typical member of the electorate, who is singled out for study.

Gini index. The Gini index is a measure of inequity that assesses the degree to which a distribution of frequencies differs from a uniform distribution of frequencies.

Hare voting system. The Hare voting procedure (for a single-winner election) requires a complete preference ranking by each voter. If no candidate obtains a majority of first-place votes, the decision rule specifies that the candidate with the fewest first-place votes is eliminated, and the second-place votes of her supporters are transferred to augment the first-place totals of the remaining candidates. This process is repeated until one candidate has a majority and is declared the winner.

Impartial culture. An impartial culture is a model of an electorate in which all preference orders (for a set of candidates) are equally likely.

Independence of irrelevant alternatives. A voting system is independent of irrelevant alternatives if the relative standings of the candidates cannot be altered by the entry of additional candidates in the race.

Insincere voting. A voter's ballot is insincere if his reported preference order differs from his true preference order.

Kemeny distance. The Kemeny distance between two preference orders is the number of adjacent pairwise switches needed to convert one preference order to the other.

Laplace method. The Laplace rule for decisions under uncertainty chooses that strategy whose expected utility is largest, where the latter is computed under the assumption that all contingencies (such as pairwise ties) are equally likely.

Monotonicity. A voting system violates monotonicity if a voter can raise a candidate in the social ordering by lowering that candidate in her individual ordering (leaving the relative ordering of other candidates unchanged) or vice versa.

Multicandidate election. A multicandidate election is an election in which there are three or more candidates.

Nash equilibrium. A Nash equilibrium constitutes a set of positions taken by participants (candidates) from which no one can benefit by deviating unilaterally.

Negative-of-distance utility. The negative-of-distance utility function specifies that a voter, at distance d from a candidate in a spatial model, have utility for that candidate given by $-d$, i.e., utility decreases linearly with distance.

Normal distribution. The normal (or Gaussian or bell-shaped) distribution of probability specifies that probability follow the density $f(x) = (1/\sigma\sqrt{2\pi}) \exp[-(x - \mu)/2\sigma^2]$.

Optimal strategy. An optimal strategy for a particular voting system is a ballot marking that optimizes an appropriate quantity, e.g., minimizes maximal regret for the Savage regret method or maximizes expected utility for the method of expected utility.

Paradox of voting. The paradox of voting occurs when transitive individual rankings by voters yield an intransitive social ranking, e.g., there exist candidates A, B, and C, such A beats B, B beats C, and C beats A.

Perceptual uncertainty of candidates' positions. In a spatial model, perceptual uncertainty of a candidate's position occurs when different voters place the candidate in different spatial positions, so that the candidate's position must be modeled by a probability distribution instead of by a point.

Permissible voting strategy. A permissible strategy for a voting system is any marking of the ballot allowed by the rules of the system.

Plunking. Plunking refers to voting for a single candidate on a ballot that permits voting for more than one.

Plurality decision rule. The plurality decision rule specifies that the candidate receiving the greatest number of votes wins. Systems using this decision rule include single-vote plurality, approval voting, and the Borda count.

Plurality voting system. See Single-vote plurality voting system.

Polarized society. A polarized society is an electorate in which two or more (usually disparate) preference orders predominate. Such a society with exactly two dominating preference orders is called a dual culture.

Preferential voting. See Hare voting system.

Random society. A random society is a model for an electorate in which, for each voter, candidate utilities are drawn independently from a uniform distribution.

Random variable. A random variable is a function that assigns to each possible outcome (of an observation or experiment) a numerical value following some probability distribution.

Relative dispersion. In a spatial model of voting, the relative dispersion of candidates to voters is the ratio of the standard deviation of the candidates' positions to that of the voters.

Runoff voting system. The runoff voting system is identical to single-vote plurality except that, if no candidate receives a majority of the votes, a second ballot is held between the two top vote-getters on the first ballot.

Savage regret. The Savage regret method for decisions under uncertainty chooses that strategy that minimizes the maximal regret that would be suffered over all contingencies (such as pairwise ties between candidates).

Shepsle utility. The Shepsle utility function specifies that a voter, at distance d from a candidate in a spatial model, have utility for that candidate given by $\exp(-d^2/2)$. This definition implies, in a bivariate normal spatial model, that the distribution of voter utilities will be approximately quadratic.

Simulation. A simulation is an experiment run as a model of reality. The simulations in this book are computer simulations, i.e., are run on a computer using mathematical models. They are also stochastic, that is they involve input generated to follow probability distributions.

Single-transferable-vote system. See the Hare voting system for single-winner elections.

Single-vote plurality voting system. The single-vote plurality voting system prescribes that each voter vote for a single candidate. The winner is the candidate with the greatest number of votes.

Social-utility efficiency. The social-utility efficiency of a voting system is the normalized ratio between the expected social utilities of the candidate selected by the system and the candidate maximizing social utility. The social utility of a candidate is the total (alternatively, the average) utility of the candidate over all voters.

Spatial model. A spatial model of voting specifies that each voter and each candidate can be placed in N-dimensional space, with each dimension representing an issue or personal characteristic. Preference orders for voters are generally determined by distances between voters and candidates.

Squeeze effect. The squeeze effect refers to the reduction in electoral suc-

137

cess of a candidate when, in a spatial model, nearby candidates draw support away from the focal candidate.

Standard deviation. Standard deviation is a measure of the variation of a random variable; namely, the square root of the average squared deviation from the mean.

Standard error of an estimate. The standard error of an estimate is the standard deviation of all estimates for a parameter based on repeated sampling for a given sample size.

Strategic voting. Strategic voting involves any decision by the voter in marking his ballot intended to improve the outcome from his point of view. In addition to insincere voting, it includes, under approval voting for example, expansion or truncation used to optimize a voter's effect on the outcome.

Transitivity. A voter's preference order is said to be transitive if whenever the voter prefers A over B and B over C, she also prefers A over C. A similar definition applies to a social preference ordering.

Von Neumann–Morgenstern utility. A rating function $u(x)$ is called a von Neumann–Morgenstern utility if for any probabilities p and q such that $p + q = 1$ and two alternatives A and B, $u(pA + qB) = pu(A) + qu(B)$. This relation is expressed in words by saying that the utility of a lottery between A and B with weights p and q is the same as the weighted average of the utilities of A and B, again using the weights p and q.

BIBLIOGRAPHY

Aldrich, J. (1975). "Candidate Support Functions in the 1968 Election: An Empirical Application of the Spatial Model." *Public Choice* 22: 1–22.

———— (1977). "Electoral Choice in 1972: A Test of Some Theorems of the Spatial Model of Electoral Competition." *Journal of Mathematical Sociology* 5: 215–37.

———— (1980). *Before the Convention.* Chicago: University of Chicago Press.

Aldrich, J., and McKelvey, R. (1977). "A Method of Scaling with Applications to the 1968 and 1972 Presidential Elections." *American Political Science Review* 71: 111–30.

Arrow, K. (1951). *Social Choice and Individual Values.* New York: Wiley.

Black, D. (1958). *The Theory of Committees and Elections.* London: Cambridge University Press.

Black, J. (1978). "The Multicandidate Calculus of Voting: Application to Canadian Federal Elections." *American Journal of Political Science* 22: 609–38.

Blair, G. S. (1973). "Cumulative Voting: An Effective Electoral Device for Fair and Minority Representation." *Annals of the New York Academy of Science* 219: 20–26.

Bogdanor, V., and Butler, D. (1983). *Democracy and Elections: Electoral Systems and Their Political Consequences.* London: Cambridge University Press.

Borda, Jean-Charles de (1781). "Mémoire sur les élections au scrutin." *Histoire de l'Académie Royale des Sciences.* Paris.

Bordley, R. F. (1983). "A Pragmatic Method for Evaluating Election Schemes through Simulation." *American Political Science Review* 77: 123–41.

Brams, S. J. (1976). "One Man, *n* Votes." Module in Applied Mathematics, Mathematical Association of America. Ithaca, NY: Cornell University.

———— (1978). *The Presidential Election Game.* New Haven: Yale University Press.

———— (1982). "Polls and the Problem of Strategic Information and Voting Behavior." *Society* 19: 4–11.

Brams, S. J. (1987). "Approval Voting and Proportional Representation." Mimeographed. New York University.

Brams, S. J., and Fishburn, P. C. (1978). "Approval Voting." *American Political Science Review* 72: 831–47.

—— (1981). "Reconstructing Voting Processes: The 1976 House Majority Leader Election." *Political Methodology* 7, 3 & 4: 95–108.

—— (1982). "Deducing Preferences and Choices in the 1980 Presidential Election." *Electoral Studies* 1: 333–46.

—— (1983). *Approval Voting.* Boston: Birkhäuser.

Brams, S. J., and Sharrard, G. (1979). "Analysis of Pilot Study Questions on Preference Rankings and Approval Voting." Mimeographed. New York University.

Brams, S. J., and Straffin, P. D., Jr. (1982). "The Entry Problem in a Political Race." In *Political Equilibrium*, ed. P. C. Ordeshook and K. A. Shepsle. Boston: Kluwer-Nijhoff, 181–95.

Brams, S. J., Urken, A., Sharrard, G., and Muzzio, D. (1981). "Results of Exit Poll of New Jersey Voters in Democratic and Republican Gubernatorial Primaries, June 2, 1981." Press release, June 17.

Cain, B. E. (1978). "Strategic Voting in Britain." *American Journal of Political Science* 22: 639–55.

Campbell, A., Converse, P., Miller, W., and Stokes, D. (1960). *The American Voter.* New York: Wiley.

Canon, B. C. (1978). "Factionalism in the South: A Test of Theory and a Revisitation of V. O. Key." *American Journal of Political Science* 22: 833–48.

Carter, C. (1987). "Admissible and Sincere Strategies under Approval Voting." Mimeographed. Trent University, Peterborough, Ontario.

Chamberlin, J. R., Cohen, J. L., and Coombs, C. H. (1984). "Social Choice Observed: Five Presidential Elections of the American Psychological Association." *Journal of Politics* 46: 479–502.

Chamberlin, J. R., and Cohen, M. D. (1978). "Toward Applicable Social Choice Theory: A Comparison of Social Choice Functions under Spatial Model Assumptions." *American Political Science Review* 72: 1341–56.

Chamberlin, J. R., and Courant, P. N. (1983). "Representative Deliberations and Representative Decisions: Proportional Representation and the Borda Rule." *American Political Science Review* 77: 718–33.

Chamberlin, J. R., and Featherston, F. (1985). "Selecting a Voting System." *Journal of Politics* 48: 347–69.

Coleman, J. S. (1982). "Social Choice among Several Mutually Exclusive Alternatives." Mimeographed. University of Chicago.

Condorcet, Marquis de (1785). *Essai sur l'application de l'analyse à la probabilité des décisions rendues à la pluralité des voix*. Paris.

Coombs, C. (1954). *Theory of Data*. New York: Wiley.

Cox, G. (1987). "Electoral Equilibrium under Alternative Voting Institutions." *American Journal of Political Science* 31: 82–108.

Dahl, R. A. (1956). *A Preface to Democratic Theory*. Chicago: University of Chicago Press.

Davis, O., Hinich, M., and Ordeshook, P. (1970). "An Expository Development of a Mathematical Model of the Electoral Process." *American Political Science Review* 64: 426–48.

De Maio, G., Muzzio, D., and Sharrard, G. (1985). "Mapping Candidate Systems Via Approval Voting." Presented at the Annual Meeting of the American Political Science Association, 29 August–1 September 1985, New Orleans, La.

Doron, G., and Kronick, R. (1977). "Single Transferable Vote: An Example of a Perverse Social Choice Function." *American Journal of Political Science* 21: 303–11.

Downs, A. (1957). *An Economic Theory of Democracy*. New York: Harper and Row.

Dutter, L. E. (1982). "The Structure of Voter Preferences: The 1921, 1925, 1973, and 1975 Northern Irish Parliamentary Elections." *Comparative Political Studies* 14: 517–42.

Duverger, M. (1963). *Political Parties: Their Organization and Activity in the Modern State*, trans. B. North and R. North. New York: Wiley.

———— (1984). "Which Is the Best Electoral System?" In *Choosing an Electoral System*, ed. A. Lijphart and B. Grofman. New York: Praeger, 31–40.

Enelow, J., and Hinich, M. (1981). "A New Approach to Voter Uncertainty in the Downsian Spatial Model." *American Journal of Political Science* 25: 483–93.

———— (1984). *The Spatial Theory of Voting*. London: Cambridge University Press.

Felsenthal, D. S., Maoz, Z., and Rapoport, A. (1985). "The Condorcet Efficiency of Sophisticated Plurality and Approval Voting." Presented at the Annual Meeting of the American Political Science Association, 29 August–1 September 1985, New Orleans, La.

Ferejohn, J. A., and Fiorina, M. P. (1975). "Closeness Counts Only in Horseshoes and Dancing." *American Political Science Review* 69: 920–25.

Fishburn, P. C. (1971). "A Comparative Analysis of Group Decision Methods." *Behavioral Science* 16: 538–44.

Fishburn, P. C. (1982). "Monotonicity Paradoxes in the Theory of Elections." *Discrete Applied Mathematics* 4: 119–34.

Fishburn, P. C., and Brams, S. J. (1981a). "Expected Utility and Approval Voting." *Behavioral Science* 26: 136–42.

——— (1981b). "Approval Voting, Condorcet's Principle, and Runoff Elections." *Public Choice* 36: 89–114.

——— (1983). "Paradoxes of Preferential Voting." *Mathematics Magazine* 56: 207–14.

Fishburn, P. C., and Gehrlein, W. (1976). "An Analysis of Simple Two-stage Voting Systems." *Behavioral Science* 21: 1–12.

——— (1977). "An Analysis of Voting Procedures with Nonranked Voting." *Behavioral Science* 22: 178–85.

Gehrlein, W. (1983). "Condorcet's Paradox." *Theory and Decision* 15: 161–97.

Gibbard, A. (1973). "Manipulation of Voting Schemes: A General Result." *Econometrica* 41: 587–601.

Hare, T. (1859). *Treatise on the Election of Representatives, Parliamentary and Municipal.* London: Longmans Green.

Harsanyi, J. (1977). *Rational Behavior and Bargaining Equilibrium in Games and Social Situations.* London: Cambridge University Press.

Hinich, M. J., and Pollard, W. (1980). "A New Approach to the Spatial Theory of Electoral Competition." *American Journal of Political Science* 25: 323–41.

Hoffman, D. (1982). "A Model for Strategic Voting." *SIAM Journal of Applied Mathematics* 42: 751–61.

——— (1983). "Relative Efficiency of Voting Systems." *SIAM Journal of Applied Mathematics* 43: 1213–19.

Joslyn, R. A. (1976). "The Impact of Decision Rules in Multicandidate Campaigns: The Case of the 1972 Democratic Presidential Nomination." *Public Choice* 25: 1–17.

Kellett, J., and Mott, K. (1977). "Presidential Primaries: Measuring Popular Choice." *Polity* 9: 528–37.

Kelly, J. S. (1978). *Arrow Impossibility Theorems.* New York: Academic Press.

Kiewiet, D. R. (1979). "Approval Voting: The Case of the 1968 Presidential Election." *Polity* 12: 170–81.

Luce, D., and Raiffa, H. (1957). *Games and Decisions.* New York: Wiley.

Ludwin, W. G. (1978). "Strategic Voting and the Borda Method." *Public Choice* 33: 85–90.

McKelvey, R. (1975). "Policy-Related Voting and Electoral Equilibrium." *Econometrica* 43: 815–43.

Mansbridge, J. J. (1983). *Beyond Adversary Democracy*. Chicago: University of Chicago Press.

Merrill, S. (1979). "Approval Voting: A 'Best Buy' Method for Multicandidate Elections?" *Mathematics Magazine* 52: 98–102.

———— (1981). "Strategic Decisions under One-State Multicandidate Voting Systems." *Public Choice* 36: 115–34.

———— (1982). "Strategic Voting in Multicandidate Elections under Uncertainty and under Risk." In *Power, Voting, and Voting Power*, ed. M. Holler. Würzburg: Physica-Verlag, 179–87.

———— (1984). "A Comparison of Efficiency of Multicandidate Electoral Systems." *American Journal of Political Science* 28: 23–48.

———— (1985). "A Statistical Model for Condorcet Efficiency Using Simulation under Spatial Model Assumptions." *Public Choice* 47: 389–403.

Merrill, S., and Nagel, J. (1987). "The Effect of Approval Balloting on Strategic Voting under Alternative Decision Rules." *American Political Science Review* 81: 509–24.

Miller, N. R. (1983). "Pluralism and Social Choice." *American Political Science Review* 77: 734–47.

Morin, R. A. *Structural Reform: Ballots*. New York: Vantage Press.

Morrison, D. F. (1976). *Multivariate Statistical Methods*. New York: McGraw-Hill.

Nagel, J. H. (1984). "A Debut for Approval Voting." *PS* 17: 62–65.

———— (1987). "The Approval Ballot as a Possible Component of Electoral Reform in New Zealand." Mimeographed. University of Pennsylvania.

Neter, J., and Wasserman, W. (1974). *Applied Linear Statistical Models*. Homewood, Ill.: Irwin.

Nie, N., and Andersen, K. (1976). "Mass Belief Systems Revisited: Political Change and Attitude Structures." In *Controversies in American Voting Behavior*, ed. R. Niemi and H. Weisberg. San Francisco: W. H. Freeman, 94–137.

Niemi, R. G. (1984). "The Problem of Strategic Behavior under Approval Voting." *American Political Science Review* 78: 952–58.

Niemi, R., and Weisberg, H. (1976). "Do Voters Think Ideologically?" In *Controversies in American Voting Behavior*, ed. R. Niemi and H. Weisberg. San Francisco: W. H. Freeman, 67–84.

Nurmi, H. (1983). "Voting Procedures: A Summary Analysis." *British Journal of Political Science* 13: 181–208.

———— (1986). "Mathematical Models of Elections and Their Relevance for Institutional Design." *Electoral Studies* 5: 167–82.

143

O'Leary, C. (1979). *Irish Elections 1918–77: Parties, Voters, and Proportional Representation*. New York: St. Martin's Press.

Oppenheimer, B. I., and Peabody, R. L. (1977). "The House Majority Leader Contest, 1976." Presented at the Annual Meeting of the American Political Science Association, 1–4 September 1977, Washington, D.C.

Penniman, H. R. (1977). *Australia at the Polls*. Washington, D.C.: American Enterprise Institute for Public Policy Research.

Poole, K. T., and Rosenthal, H. (1984). "U.S. Presidential Elections 1968–80: A Spatial Analysis." *American Journal of Political Science* 28: 282–312.

Rabushka, A., and Shepsle, K. (1972). *Politics in Plural Societies: A Theory of Democratic Instability*. Columbus, Oh.: Charles E. Merrill.

Rae, D. (1971). *The Political Consequences of Election Laws*. New Haven: Yale University Press.

Riker, W. (1982a). *Liberalism against Populism*. San Francisco: W. H. Freeman.

——— (1982b). "The Two-party System and Duverger's Law: An Essay on the History of Political Science." *American Political Science Review* 76: 753–66.

Riker, W., and Ordeshook, P. (1973). *An Introduction to Positive Political Theory*. Englewood Cliffs, N.J.: Prentice-Hall.

Rosenstone, S. (1983). *Forecasting Presidential Elections*. New Haven: Yale University Press.

Satterthwaite, M. (1975). Strategy-proofness and Arrow's Conditions: Existence and Correspondence Theorems for Voting Procedures and Social Welfare Functions." *Journal of Economic Theory* 10: 187–217.

Shepsle, K. A. (1972). "Parties, Voters, and the Risk Environment: A Mathematical Treatment of Electoral Competition under Uncertainty." In *Probability Models of Collective Decision Making*, ed. R. Niemi and H. Weisberg. Columbus, Oh.: Charles E. Merrill, 273–97.

Snider, G. A. (1979). "Assessing the Candidate Preference Function." *American Journal of Political Science* 23: 732–54.

Straffin, P. D. (1980). *Topics in the Theory of Voting*. Boston: Birkhäuser.

Tideman, T. N. (1981). "The Relative Attractiveness of Voting Rules." Presented at the Annual Meeting of the Public Choice Society, 13–15 March 1981, New Orleans, La.

Weber, R. J. (1977). "Comparison of Voting Systems." New Haven: Cowles Foundation Discussion paper no. 498A.

Young, H. P. (1975). "Social Choice Scoring Functions." *SIAM Journal of Applied Mathematics* 28: 824–38.

INDEX

ABC News, exit-poll, 91, 94
abortion, 30
abstention, 18, 125
adjusted Borda count, 58n
admissible strategy, 52, 61n, 69, 100
adversary democracy, xvi
Aldrich, John, 19, 22, 41
Alessandri, Jorge, 4
alienation, 18
Allende, Salvadore, 4–5
alternative vote, 13. *See also* Hare voting
system
alternative voting systems, xv, 4, 6, 8–9.
See also specific voting systems
American National Election Study, 19, 70–
73, 90–91
American Psychological Association, president of, 19; use of Hare system in, 73–
75, 77
Anderson, John, 47
approval voting, xv, 12n, 16–18, 74, 98;
Condorcet efficiency of, 18–21, 24–28,
39–46, 74–75, 111–13; definition of, 12;
empirical estimates for, 70–76, 89–95;
optimal strategies under, 53, 57–59,
117–18; relation to candidate mean position, 43n–44n; social utility efficiency of,
32–37; strategic voting under, 47, 64,
67–70, 72–88, 90–91, 121–24, 128
Arrow's axioms, 10, 96–99
Arrow's impossibility theorem, 9–11, 104
Askew, Reuben, 94
Australia, xv, 3, 107; House of Representatives, 13; Senate, 13n

Baker, Howard, 91–92, 95
balloting method, xv, 11–14
ballot-threshold rules, 82–88, 121–24
Bayes method. *See* Laplace method
Bell, John, 5, 8
Bentham's method. *See* cardinal-measure
voting
Black, Duncan, 14, 58n

Black, Jerome, 51
Black voting system, 4, 11, 14–15, 98;
Condorcet efficiency of, 18–21, 24–28;
social utility efficiency of, 32–37; strategic voting under, 66, 77
Bolling, Richard, 3–4
Borda, Jean-Charles de, 12
Borda count, xv, 4, 11–12, 14, 74, 98;
Condorcet efficiency of, 18–21, 24–28,
39–46, 74–75, 111–13; empirical esti-
mates for, 73–75; optimal strategies un-
der, 53, 58–59, 117, 119, 128–29; social
utility efficiency of, 32–37; strategic vot-
ing under, 48, 64, 67–69, 72–78, 128–
29. *See also* adjusted Borda count
Bordley, Robert, 34
Bradley, Tom, 5
Brams, Steven, xvi, 12, 81, 100; rules for
strategic voting, 64–69, 76, 121–22
Breckinridge, John C., 5
Britain, xv, 8, 12, 51
broad support, 5–6
bullet-voting. *See* plunking
Burton, Philip, 3–4
Bush, George, 91–92
Byrne, Jane, 5

Cain, Bruce, 51
Canada, xv, 8, 12
candidate mean, 44n
Canon, B. C., 8–9
cardinal-measure voting, 50, 59, 72–73,
102, 128
Carter, Cyril, 61n
CBS/New York Times poll, 19
centrifugal force, 27
centripetal force, 27
centrist candidate, xvi, 4–5, 7, 11, 27–28,
40–41, 106, 112
Chamberlin, John, 18n, 19, 21, 24–25, 73–
75
Chicago, mayor of, 5
Chile, 1970 presidential election, 4–5

145

non-imposition, 10, 96
normal distribution: bivariate, 22–23, 114,
   121; multivariate, 17, 21–25, 39, 41,
   109; mixture of, 40
Northern Ireland, xv
Nurmi, Hannu, 18n

optimal strategies, 11, 17, 28, 47–63, 96,
   102, 117; under approval voting, 47, 79,
   121–24; under the Borda count, 48–49;
   effect on Condorcet efficiency of, 64–78;
   for equiprobable outcomes, 35, 53, 62,
   72; under single-vote plurality, 47; vote-
   for-half strategy, 48, 93. *See also* decisions; potentially uniquely optimal strategies
Ordeshook, Peter, 18
ordinal preferences. *See* preference order

paradox of voting, 9n, 35n
partial culture (dual culture), 17n, 40
payoff matrix, 52–53
Pennsylvania State Democratic Committee,
   use of approval voting, 81, 92–94
perceptual uncertainty of candidates' positions, 29, 38–41, 44–45, 105
plunking, 58, 81, 87–88, 92–93, 121–24
plurality decision rule, 11, 28, 49–50, 56–
   59, 96, 125; effect of strategic voting,
   67–68. *See also* single-vote plurality voting system
polarization, 5, 39–40, 45
polling data, 10, 19, 81, 90–94; effect on
   strategic voting, 64–67, 70–73, 87, 121–
   24; simulation of polls, 67–70
Poole, Keith, 44, 56n
populist interpretation of voting, 6
potentially uniquely optimal strategies, 99–
   101, 125–30
preference order, xv, 7, 9n, 12–13, 16–17,
   19, 25, 65, 69, 100
preferential vote, 13. *See also* Hare voting
   system
primary election, 5, 27, 71, 89. *See also*
   U. S. presidential election
probability: conditional, 54, 60; relative,
   54, 56n, 62n, 68, 71, 80, 83
proliferation of candidates. *See* factionalism

proportional representation, 6n, 9, 13n
pushover, 67, 75, 88, 97, 105

random-society model, 16–22, 24–25, 32–
   35, 104
ranking of candidates. *See* preference order
Rapoport, Amnon, 69
Reagan, Ronald, 91
regression, logistic multiple, 38, 39n, 44–
   45, 109–13
regret matrix, 52–53
relative dispersion. *See* dispersion, relative
relative likelihood. *See* probability, relative
Republican Party, 48–49, 81, 91–92
Riker, William, xvi, 5–6, 9–10, 18
Rosenthal, Howard, 18, 22n
runoff, xvi, 4, 8–9, 11, 13, 98, 104–107;
   combined with approval balloting, 82;
   Condorcet efficiency of, 18–21, 24–28,
   39–46, 111–13; social utility efficiency
   of, 32–37; strategic voting under, 65–66,
   77; violation of monotonicity under, 97

Satterthwaite, Mark Allan, xvii
Savage regret, 51, 53, 62, 117–19
Senate, U. S., 13
shared support, under approval voting, 89,
   94
Sharrard, George, 81, 94
Shepsle, Kenneth. *See* utility, Shepsle
Shriver, Sargent, 71–72
simplicity, 4, 8, 107
simulation. *See* computer simulation
sincere voting, levels of under approval voting: decapitation, 80, 82, 87; pure sincerity, 80, 121; skipping, 48, 61n, 79–80,
   82, 88, 105; truncation/expansion, 75,
   80, 87–88, 105, 121, 123
single-transferable-vote system, 13. *See also*
   Hare voting system
single-vote plurality voting system, xv, xvii,
   3, 6n, 7–9, 11–12, 74–75, 98, 104–107;
   Condorcet efficiency of, 18–21, 24–28,
   39–46, 74–75, 95, 111–13; empirical estimates for, 70–76, 89–92, 95; as a minimal voting system, 99–101; optimal
   strategies under, 53, 58–59, 117–18,
   128; social utility efficiency of, 32–37;
   strategic voting under, 47, 64, 67–70,

72–78, 128; violation of independence of irrelevant alternatives under, 73, 98–99
single-winner elections, 4, 9
Snider, G. A., 80, 114
social-choice theory, xv, xvii, 9n, 10
social utility, 7, 20, 24, 37, 104; definition of, 32; efficiency (SUE), 30–46, 104–107; under strategic voting, 64
sophisticated voting, 64, 69–70, 77
southern United States, elections in, 9, 13
spatial model, 104; for Condorcet efficiency, 16–29, 38–45, 70, 109–13; definition of, 16; for new entries, 98–99; for social utility efficiency, 34–36, 38; for strategic voting, 70; symmetric, 25, 27–28
squeeze effect, 4–5, 27, 40–41, 45, 104, 112; effect on Condorcet efficiency, 51; relation to independence of irrelevant alternatives, 98; effect on social utility efficiency, 37
stability, 4, 8
standard deviation, 19n, 22, 41, 101, 130
standard error, 19n, 34n
standard-score voting system, 101–103, 130–31
Straffin, Philip, xvi
strategic value, 56–60, 62, 68, 100, 130
strategic voting, 7, 46–78, 104–107. See also decisions; optimal strategies
strategy, permissible, 50, 99–100, 120, 125–30
successive elimination, 3, 13
symmetric spatial distribution, 106

thermometer scores, 19, 70–71, 90
threshold. See ballot-threshold rules; vote-threshold rules
Tideman, Nicolaus, 61, 61n, 70, 74
ties, resolution of, 21n, 52, 54, 60, 80
Tomic, Radomiro Romero, 4
transitive ranking, 9, 9n
two-party system, 7–8

two-stage decision rules under approval balloting, 82–88

uniform distribution, 16, 28, 39–40, 45
unitary democracy, xvi
United Nations, use of approval voting for Secretary General of, 92
urban unrest, 41
Urken, Arnold, 81
U. S. National Academy of Sciences, use of approval voting, 92
U. S. presidential election, 19–22; of 1860, 5, 8; of 1964, 5; of 1968, 18, 22n, 41, 90–91; of 1972, 5, 41, 47, 71–73, 92; of 1976, 18–19, 22n, 81; of 1980, 47, 81, 91; of 1984, 92–94
utility, 7, 7n, 16, 25, 31, 49, 96; expected, 16n, 51, 55–56, 99–100, 102–103, 117, 120, 125–26; expressed as a function, 17, 38, 42, 44, 114–16; interpersonal comparison of, 31, 32n; mean-utility cutpoint, 53, 57, 59–62, 79–81; negative-of-distance, 42–45, 115–16, 122; negative skew of voters, 80, 87, 123; normalized by range, 34n; normalized by standard scores, 34n; Shepsle, 39, 42–45, 114–16, 121–22; Von Neumann-Morgenstern, 31, 61

Vietnam, 41
vote-threshold rules, 82–88
voting system, definition of, 11

Wallace, George, 47, 71–73, 90–91, 95
Washington, Harold, 5
Weber, Robert, 32, 34n, 53, 99
Weibull distribution, 114
Weisberg, Herbert, 18
winning-oriented candidates, 28
Wright, Jim, 3–4

Young, Andrew, 5
Young, Coleman, 5

LIBRARY OF CONGRESS
Library of Congress Cataloging-in-Publication Data

Merrill, Samuel, 1939–
Making multicandidate elections more democratic / Samuel Merrill, III.

p.   cm.   Bibliography: p.   Includes index.
ISBN 0–691–07770–3 (alk. paper)
1. Voting—Mathematical models. 2. Political science—Decision making—
Mathematical models. 3. Game theory. I. Title.
JF1001.M47 1988
328′.3347—dc19   87–25856
                                                                CIP

SAMUEL MERRILL, III is Professor of Mathematics and
Computer Science at Wilkes College.